The Complete Guide to Facebook Advertising

TABLE OF CONTENTS

Table of contents   2

Ackowledgements   6

Introduction   9

Chapter 1: The Whats and the Whys of Facebook Advertising   11
    Paid Social vs. Paid Search   11
    What Is a Facebook Ad?   16

Chapter 2: Important Terms   20

Chapter 3: Getting Started   25
    Creating a Facebook Profile   25
    Creating a Facebook Page   29
    Creating a Business Manager Account   34

Chapter 4: Boosted Posts, the Ad for Beginners   36

Chapter 5: Understanding Business Manager, Ads Manager, and Power Editor   40
    Business Manager   40
    Ads Manager   76
    Power Editor   84

Chapter 6: Ad Account Setup   86
    Connecting with Your Partner   86
    Creating a New Ad Account   93

Granting Permissions to Ad Accounts and Pages 95

Setting Up Your Facebook Pixel 99

Chapter 7: Creating Facebook Ads **125**

Choosing an Objective 126

Creating Your Target Audience 133

Choosing Your Ad Placements 154

Choosing Your Budget and Schedule 166

Choosing a Page 173

Adding Your Media, Text, Links, and Pixel 182

Chapter 8: Creating Special Ads **185**

Lead Ads 185

Dynamic Product Ads 200

Slideshow Ads 210

Canvas Ads 215

Collection Ads 220

App Install Ads 226

Offers Ads 246

Chapter 9: Facebook Ad Guidelines and Policies **251**

Prohibited Content 252

Restricted Content 257

Video Ads 259

Targeting 260

Positioning 260

Text in Images 261

Lead Ads 261

Use of Our Brand Assets 264

Data Use Restrictions 264

Things You Should Know 265

Chapter 10: Managing Your Facebook Page   **267**

     Updating Your Settings   267

     Adding an Instagram Account   273

     Blocking Words and Profanity   276

     Adding Features and Followers   279

     Important Page Tools   288

Chapter 11: Facebook Resources   **295**

     Best Digital Advertising Blogs   295

     Contact Links   299

     Messenger Bots   300

Chapter 12: The Psychology of Facebook Ads   **303**

     The Five Ps of Marketing and Other Elements   303

     Evoking Emotions   306

     The Psychological Impact of Colors   310

Chapter 13: Creative Best Practices   **312**

     Copy   312

     Images   315

     People and Objects   316

     Video   318

     Incorporate the Three Es   319

Afterword   **321**

Glossary   **323**

About the Author   **369**

FREE
FACEBOOK AD TARGETING GUIDE

Download a FREE Facebook ad targeting guide with over 850 ad targeting options to help ensure you're targeting your Facebook ads correctly.

advertisemint.com/complete-guide-facebook-ad-targeting

ACKOWLEDGEMENTS

Although it was difficult to write this book because Facebook advertising changes so often, the project prevailed thanks to the amazing team that helped bring it to completion. I would like to thank the following individuals who helped bring this book into existence.

Anne Felicitas, Editor

This book exists because of you. Thank you for meticulously editing this book, providing content and screenshots, and reading and replying to the thousands of emails I sent your way. Thank you.

Chad, Spencer, and Arjun, Facebook Representatives

Without the knowledge and guidance you provided through detailed explanations, conference calls, emails, and screen sharing sessions that helped my team understand the inner workings of Facebook's ad platform, this book would not have the cutting-edge knowledge of Facebook's ad system, so thank you.

The AdvertiseMint Team

I am so blessed to work with an amazing team whose skills and talents I often brag about to others. My team and I enjoy the spoils of victory and work hard at the office while smiling and laughing together. My team, you were all an integral part of this book's creation. Thank you.

Arnold and Laura Meert, My Parents

You told me to always do my best. That wonderful nugget of wisdom has paid dividends over my life. This book is a testament to all the ways you have invested in my education, my future, and my experiences, which gave me the confidence to become an expert in my industry.

John Thomas, Dean of Business, La Sierra University

You were the first person who challenged me to start a business. Within a few weeks, I had majestically failed at multiple tasks, but you challenged me to try again. Thousands of tries later, I'm now an expert who is helping others to grow their business by giving it a try.

Clients

When my agency first began, there was a time when cash flow was extremely tight. However, there were a few company executives who believed in AdvertiseMint, executives who gave me and my team the chance to grow their business. I want to repay their faith in my company by sharing their business information below. I highly recommend the products, services, and events they offer.

American Bullion[1]

My very first client, American Bullion helps individuals transfer traditional investments from a 401(k) or IRA into physical gold or silver. Their friendly team will walk you through the entire process.

---

1   www.americanbullion.com

Newegg[2]

The leading online store to buy electronics, Newegg sells computers, laptops, games, and drones, among many others, for the techie in your life.

NatoMounts[3]

If you have a cell phone or a tablet, you'll want this mount. I have one in my car, bathroom, office, garage, and shower—you can use this mount wherever you are.

Malibu Half Marathon & 5K Run/Walk[4]

If you run one race this year, it should be the Malibu Half Marathon, the most scenic half marathon in the United States. This wonderfully organized event takes place in Malibu with its near perfect weather and beautiful view of the ocean. The first year I ran this, I saw dolphins in the water, and it was just an amazing experience.

WaiveCar[5]

This Santa Monica start-up rents electric cars to customers for free for the first two hours and then for $4.99 after that.

---

2   www.newegg.com

3   www.natomounts.com

4   www.malibumarathon.com

5   www.waivecar.com

INTRODUCTION

The first day I saw Facebook's advertising platform in 2014, I instantly knew it was an advertising revolution. I was impressed by the massive data Facebook collected from each user, data that it uses for its never-before-seen laser-precision ad targeting. It was incredible. After seeing the potential of Facebook's ad targeting tools, the first of its kind, I went home that day and created AdvertiseMint, a digital advertising agency that specializes in social media advertising.

After several years of managing Facebook ads full time, I can tell you that Facebook advertising is very different from traditional or other forms of digital advertising. For one, unlike traditional advertising, Facebook advertising requires constant supervision. When my grandfather needed to promote his air-conditioning business in Miami in the '60s, all he needed to do was create an ad in the yellow pages and then sit back and wait for customers—he was done for the entire year. Facebook ads don't work that way. With Facebook ads, I had to check on all of my clients' accounts and create new ads almost every day. Times have changed—you can't use old, traditional advertising methods and expect them to work with Facebook ads.

Additionally, unlike traditional advertising, managing Facebook ads requires extensive knowledge of social media, technology, and Facebook's advertising website, Business Manager, and the dashboards within it, Ads Manager and Power Editor. However, the results are worth the headache that comes with understanding Facebook advertising. Whether you're the owner of a Fortune 500 company or a start-up launching a crowdfunding campaign, you will be able to grow and strengthen your business with Facebook advertising. This book is for people like you, people who want to grow their businesses but who are confused about the platform. Before you proceed to the first chapter, however, there are a few things you need to know about this book.

1. This book is user friendly.

Because advertising on Facebook can be a complicated process, I wrote this book using the language, explanations, and illustrations that even my mother could understand. Although Facebook advertising can be a tricky and confusing subject, I promise that if you stay with me, you'll be running Facebook ads like a pro.

2. This book is concise.

I respect your time. You probably have millions of other things on your plate, and reading hundreds of pages may be the last thing you want to add to your already busy schedule. My editor and I have trimmed the content down to only the essentials needed to help you become an expert in Facebook advertising in the shortest amount of time possible.

I've delayed your Facebook advertising lesson long enough.
Let's get right to it.

CHAPTER 1:
THE WHATS AND THE WHYS OF FACEBOOK ADVERTISING

Paid Social vs. Paid Search

In 1836, the French newspaper *La Presse* included paid advertising in its pages, increasing profitability and lowering the cost of the paper, which attracted more readers. Newspaper advertising was quickly followed by billboards in 1835, radio commercials in the 1920s, and TV commercials in 1941. By 2000, after the advent of the Internet, ads started appearing in the World Wide Web, the first development of digital advertising and the precursor to social media advertising. A type of digital advertising, Facebook advertising is often referred to as social media advertising because the ads appear within its social media platform. It is also considered to be paid social marketing.

One of the most common questions I receive from aspiring young advertisers, their eyes glimmering with ambition, is what is the difference between paid search, such as Google Adwords and Bing Ads, and paid social, such as Facebook and Instagram ads? The difference between these two is the audience's intent. With paid search, you advertise within search engines such as Google, Bing, and Yahoo, and you pay every time a prospective buyer clicks on your ad or every time your ad is displayed. A search is the only way your prospective customers will find your ad. They type the keywords of the desired item or service into the search engine, and once the keywords match your ad's, it will appear in the search results. That is not the case with paid social. In fact, there is no way prospective customers can search for your ad. Rather, your ads will appear in social media platforms, an area where your customers are socializing and sharing content with friends and family. Unlike the audience of paid search, the audience of paid social has zero purchase intent.

Facebook as a paid social has probably instilled some doubt in you. "If, as a Facebook advertiser, my audience has no purchase intent, how am I supposed to sell anything," you exclaim, spewing your morning coffee. Don't despair. There are ten reasons why Facebook is effective, reasons that, I'm sure, will dissolve all of your doubts.

1. Facebook has a massive audience.

As of 2017, Facebook has over 2.01 billion monthly users—that's 2.01 billion potential customers. Facebook has not only a large audience but also the highest user activity. Currently, Facebook is the most popular social media networking service. Data from *Pew Research Center* shows that 70 percent of US Facebook users access the site daily, and 43 percent of the 70 percent access it multiple times a day. Additionally, 82 percent of eighteen- to twenty-nine-year-olds are active Facebook users.[6] With this many users, you have a higher chance of reaching your target audience.

---

6   Amanda Lenhart, Kristen Purcell, Aaron Smith, and Kathryn Zickuhr, "Part 3: Social Media," Pew Research Center: Internet, Science & Tech., February 2, 2010, accessed July 14, 2017, http://www.pewinternet.org/2010/02/03/part-3-social-media/.

2. Facebook has laser-precision targeting.

Traditional advertising on the radio and in print works well if you want to target a local audience; for instance, a radio ad can only play within the radius of a tower. Similarly, mailbox flyers will only reach households close to your business. Facebook ads aren't limited by those restrictions. You can send an ad anywhere in the world. Additionally, Facebook advertising has what most forms of traditional advertising don't have: eerily specific laser-precision targeting. You can target an audience with specific lifestyles, behaviors, demographics, and interests. For example, a company selling electronics can target single men aged eighteen to thirty living within a five-mile radius of 312 Arizona Avenue, Santa Monica, in an apartment, with an annual salary of $50,000. Yes, like I said, *eerily specific*. By targeting an audience with specific traits that you define, you can target an audience that is most likely interested in your business.

3. Facebook is cost effective.

Unless your company is as big as Coke or Nike, traditional advertising may be too expensive for you. On average, local television stations charge from $200 to $1,500 for a thirty-second commercial. Meanwhile, print advertising can range from $500 to $20,000. With traditional advertising, it's difficult to internationally spread brand awareness unless you have a substantial amount of money stowed away somewhere. Facebook advertising, in contrast, is so cost effective that even small businesses, start-ups, and mom-and-pop shops can afford it. Facebook's cost per click (CPC), on average, is around sixty-one cents.

4. Facebook has a powerful audience insights tool.

When you advertise on Facebook, you'll have access to audience insights. Audience insights provide you with real-time information about the people who interacted with your ad, including their geography, lifestyle, demographics, and purchase behavior. You can then use the information from audience insights to improve your campaigns by adjusting your target audience, budget, and placements.

5. Facebook reaches a huge mobile audience.

According to a *Time* article, Facebook, Messenger, and Facebook-owned Instagram are listed in the top ten most frequently downloaded mobile apps in the world.[7] Because more people access social media through mobile phones rather than through desktops, it's important that social media companies garner a large mobile audience.

6. Facebook allows you to target loyal, high-intent customers.

Custom audience is a Facebook advertising feature that allows you to advertise to specific Facebook users in your already existing customer list. Once you upload your customer list to Facebook, Facebook will match the first and last names, email addresses, and phone numbers of your customers from your list to existing Facebook users. Facebook will then serve ads to the matched individuals.

---

7   Lisa Eadicicco, "These Are the Most Popular iPhone Apps of 2016," Time, December 6, 2016, accessed July 17, 2017. http://time.com/4592864/most-popular-iphone-apps-2016/.

7. Facebook lets you increase your best customers.

Once you've uploaded your custom audience to Facebook, you can target ads to users who are similar to the customers in your customer list by creating a lookalike audience. In doing so, you're expanding an audience most likely interested in your business.

8. Facebook lets you advertise on multiple platforms.

Facebook allows you to advertise on its mobile news feed, desktop news feed, and right column. You can also advertise outside of Facebook, such as through the Instagram feed, Instagram Stories (because Facebook owns Instagram), and the audience network, a network of partners that allow you to advertise through their apps and websites. Advertising on multiple platforms allows you to not only reach a wider audience but also lower placements costs. For example, if the CPCs for Facebook are more expensive for your ad, you can advertise on the alternative options, whether that's on the Audience Network, Instagram feed, or Instagram Stories.

9. Facebook lets you A/B test everything.

Facebook allows you to test one ad element against another: you can test copy against copy, images against images, audience against audience, and demographics against demographics. With fast, real-time results, A/B testing allows you to improve and perfect your ad.

10. Facebook lets you collect users' information with lead ads.

Lead ads, which often include a call-to-action button that says "subscribe" or "sign up," are ads that provide a quick and easy way for users to give contact information. Once users have clicked the button, they will be redirected to a mobile-friendly form that automatically fills in the information they provided on Facebook.

Lead ads are beneficial because they accommodate users who are often busy and on the go. Not only do they allow users to type less, but they also provide businesses with accurate, actionable information. Most important, they allow you to connect with an audience that is interested in your products or services.

There are multiple benefits to Facebook advertising. If I've convinced you, perhaps you would be interested in knowing the three types of Facebook ads that exist.

What Is a Facebook Ad?

In traditional advertising, there are several types of ads you can use. You can use TV ads, radio ads, and print ads, just to name a few. Different ad types also exist in Facebook advertising. For instance, you have sponsored stories that appear in Facebook's news feed, and you have Facebook ads that appear on all placements. It's also important to mention that because Facebook owns Instagram, Instagram ads are also a part of Facebook advertising. You create Instagram ads through Facebook's ad creation dashboards, Ads Manager or Power Editor, and you can even place Facebook news feed ads in Instagram's feed without having to make additional adjustments to your creative. In this section, I discuss the different types of Facebook ads.

Sponsored Stories

First, you have sponsored stories, content created by users' interaction with a business's status update. Let's say you posted an image of your product, and one of your followers shared it. Delighted to receive this type of engagement, you paid Facebook to highlight that follower's action. By paying Facebook, that regular engagement post turns into an ad that appears in the news feed.

Figure 1.1
A sponsored story

Ads

Next, you have ads that you create in one of Facebook's ad-creation dashboards, Power Editor or Ads Manager. When you create these ads, you have the power to choose your objective, your budget, your target audience, your ad format, and your creatives. You can place your ads on Facebook, Instagram, or in the Audience Network, a network comprising partners who allow Facebook advertisers to advertise in their apps and websites.

Figure 1.2
A news feed ad

Boosted Posts

Finally, you have boosted posts, which are regular posts that you pay to show to an audience with the targeting that you define. Whereas regular posts only appear once to your followers' news feeds, boosted posts appear to a target audience you choose, even an audience that isn't your followers. The boosted post will repeatedly appear in your audience's feed like an ad for the amount of time that you choose. To create a boosted post, you must post a status update on your Facebook page and pay Facebook to turn it into an ad, an action referred to as boosting.

Figure 1.3
A boosted post

Stories

Stories ads are ten- to fifteen-second full-screen vertical video ads that appear between Instagram users' Stories, videos or photos that disappear from the Stories bar after twenty-four hours. Although this type of ad is only exclusive to Instagram, you can only create it in Facebook's Ads Manager. Much like Instagram, Facebook, too, has its own version of Stories, although it is not yet monetized.

Figure 1.4
An Instagram Stories ad

So far you know the difference between traditional advertising and digital advertising, paid search and paid social, the benefits of Facebook advertising, and the different types of Facebook ads that exist—all information you need to know to become a Facebook advertiser. Now you need to know a few important Facebook terms.

CHAPTER 2: IMPORTANT TERMS

Throughout this book, I'll be using Facebook advertising jargon that you might not understand, words such as "news feed," "user," and "objective"; these are words that every Facebook advertiser must know. This chapter is dedicated to a few common Facebook advertising terms. If, as you read this book, you stumble upon a term that isn't listed here, you can refer to the glossary.

Audience Network

A partnership between Facebook and several app and website owners that allows you to place ads in the websites and apps of Facebook's partners. Partners include the Huffington Post and the Cut the Rope app.

Bid

The amount you're willing to pay to display your ad.

Call-to-Action (CTA) Buttons

Buttons that urge users to perform a desired action, whether that action is to learn more, sign up, shop now, or call now. Available on every Facebook ad, these buttons will send users to a landing page or, if your ad is a lead ad, to a prefilled form.

Figure 2.1
The CTA button is located on the bottom right corner of the ad

Cost Per Acquisition (CPA)

An online advertising pricing method in which you pay for each specified acquisition (or action). For example, you can choose to pay $5 an impression, click, form submit, or sale. Depending on your budget, you can adjust the price you would like to pay per acquisition. In a CPA pricing method, you must first know the objectives you want to achieve and therefore the acquisition you want to pay for and the amount you're willing to pay for each acquisition.

Engagement

The actions that occur on an ad, such as likes, shares, comments, views, and clicks.

Facebook Pixel

A piece of JavaScript code that tracks web visitors' actions on your website.

Frequency

The average number of times Facebook showed your ad to a user

Native Advertising

A type of disguised online advertising in which marketers create ads that match the look, tone, and function of regular, unpaid posts. Native ads, unlike sidebar ads, appear inside the news feed, among posts by friends and family. News feed ads, the hardest Facebook ads to distinguish from unpaid posts, are an example of native ads. You will know that a post is an ad if it's labeled as "sponsored" underneath the publisher's name. Otherwise, news feed ads look similar to regular posts.

Figure 2.2 A regular post on the left and a native ad on the right

News Feed

The constantly updating list of posts, status updates, and ads in the middle of your home page.

Negative Feedback

Negative feedback is the number of times users make an unwanted action such as hiding your ads, choosing not to see ads from you, or reporting your ads as spam. If you have a low amount of positive feedback, you will have a low relevance score.

Objective

Your ad's goal. Objectives include clicks, conversions, engagement, page likes, app installs, app engagement, and video views.

Optimized Bidding

A bidding type that allows advertisers to optimize a bid and delivery for a specific objective (or goal).

Placement

The area where your ad appears. Placement options include desktop news feed, mobile news feed, right column, Instagram feed, Instagram Stories, Audience Network, and in-stream videos.

Positive Feedback

The number of times your target audience makes a desired action, whether that's sharing, liking, or converting. If you have a high amount of positive feedback, you will have a high relevance score.

Reach

The number of users who have seen your ad. Be wary, however, because the number of users reached that Facebook gives you is misleading; it counts the number of people who have seen your ad and the number of times those people have seen your ad. For example, if one person has seen your ad twice, Facebook will record that as two for reach.

Relevance Score

A metric that estimates your ad's relevance to its target audience in real time. The more relevant an ad is to your audience, the better it's likely to perform. Ads with high relevance scores are shown to your target more often than ads with low relevance scores. Facebook represents your ads' relevance score with a rating of one to ten, one being the least relevant and ten being the most relevant. Facebook determines whether your ad is relevant to your audience by weighing its positive and negative feedback.

Targeting

A set of specific descriptions you use to describe an audience you want to show your ads to. Targeting is usually a combination of interests, behaviors, demographics, and locations that you define.

User

A person who regularly uses social media networking sites such as Facebook, Snapchat, Twitter, or Instagram. In this book, I often refer to people who frequent social media and who see and interact with your ads as users.

CHAPTER 3: GETTING STARTED

To advertise on Facebook, you must have access to its advertising website called Business Manager. However, to register for a Business Manager account, you must first register for a Facebook account and create a Facebook page. This chapter guides you through the process of creating a Facebook profile, Facebook page, and a Business Manager account.

Creating a Facebook Profile

Creating a Facebook profile takes less than five minutes, and it is the first step needed to advertise on Facebook. Facebook requires that all advertising be done from a user account. Follow these steps to set up a profile.

Step 1: Go to www.facebook.com >> enter the information >> click "Sign Up"
It's important that you use an email that you frequently check when registering for a Facebook account because that will be the email that receives important notifications about your ad campaigns.

Step 2: Click "Edit Profile"

Step 3: Click "Add Photo"

Step 4: Click "Upload Photo"

Step 5: Choose a photo >> click "Open"

Step 6: Reposition photo >> click "Save"

Step 7: You're done

Creating a Facebook Page

The next step is creating a Facebook page. It's important to own a Facebook page because it will be the account that represents your ads. Without a page, you cannot access Business Manager and create ads.

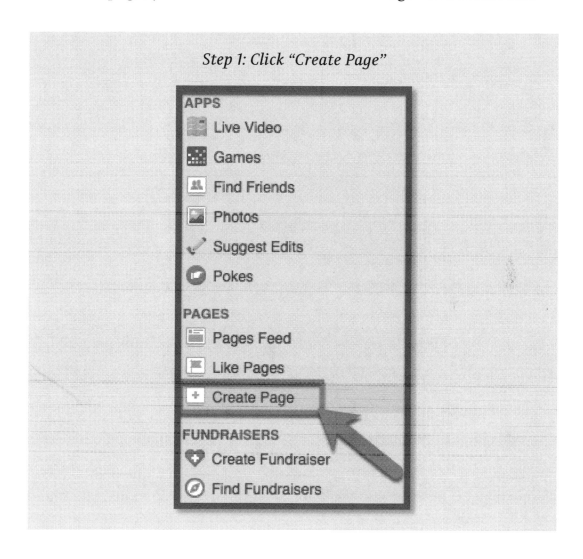

Step 1: Click "Create Page"

Step 2: Choose page type

Choose the page type that represents your entity. If you own a local business (i.e., you only have one store or office) choose "**Local Business or Place.**" If you're representing a brand, such as Coke, Nike, or Forever 21, with multiple brick-and-mortar stores, choose "**Brand or Product.**"

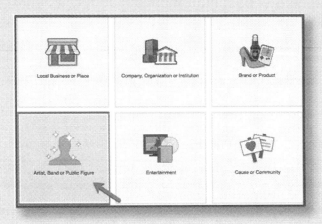

Step 3: Fill in information >> click "Get Started"

Step 4: Add description >> click "Save Info"

The description should encapsulate your entity. If your page represents a business, describe what kind of business it is. What services or products do you offer?

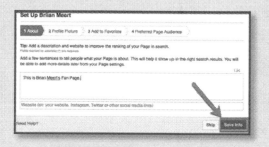

Step 5: Click "Upload From Computer"

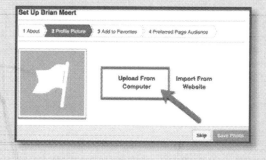

Step 6: Choose photo and then click "Next"

Step 7: Click "Add to Favorites"

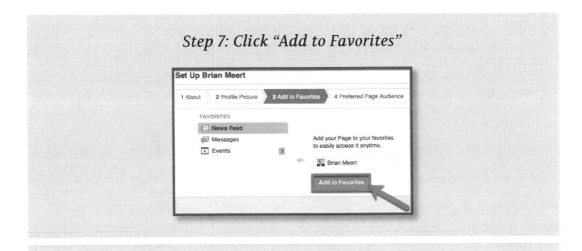

Step 8: Click "Next"

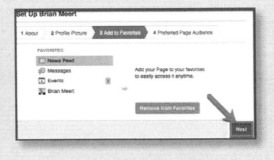

Step 9: Choose a preferred audience >> Save

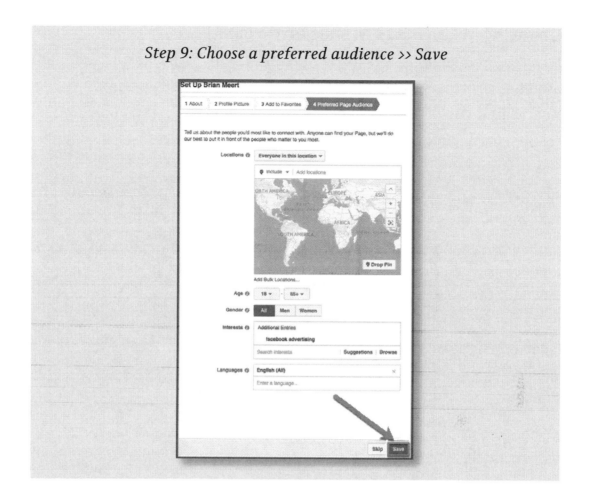

After creating your page, take a few minutes to develop it by adding a cover photo that represents your business and business information such as business hours and phone number. Once you've developed your page, you're ready to create a Business Manager account.

Creating a Business Manager Account

Business Manager is the website that allows you to create ads and manage, control, and share ad accounts, pages, and other assets. Everything you do as a Facebook advertiser—creating ads, analyzing results, managing your campaigns—must be done here.

Step 1: Business.facebook.com >> "Create Account"

Step 2: Add business name

Type in your business name and then click "Continue"

Step 3: Create your profile >> Click "Finish"

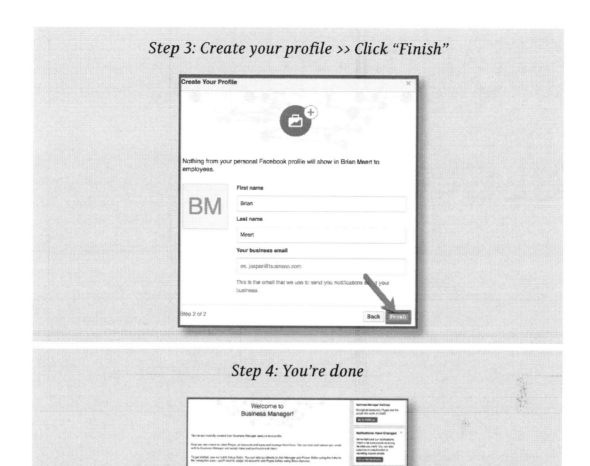

Step 4: You're done

CHAPTER 4: BOOSTED POSTS, THE AD FOR BEGINNERS

In the introduction, I briefly talked about boosted posts—that is, regular Facebook posts that you boost (or pay) to show to a targeted audience. Although Facebook advertising experts don't normally use boosted posts, most advertisers completely new to Facebook advertising begin with them. Because of the simplicity and ease of boosted posts, novices, who don't have the expertise to navigate through Ads Manager or Power Editor, begin with them before dabbling with the more complex ads.

Learning to boost a post is a great precursor to learning to create Facebook ads. You can practice not only creating a target audience but also setting a budget and writing ad copies. Although boosting a post is a great start for beginners, remember that boosted posts are just that—a great start. If you want to run professional and successful ads for the long-term, you should treat boosted posts as the training wheels, the stepping stones to Facebook ads. So before we dabble with Facebook ads, let's get you started with a boosted post.

Step 1: Create regular page post >> boost post

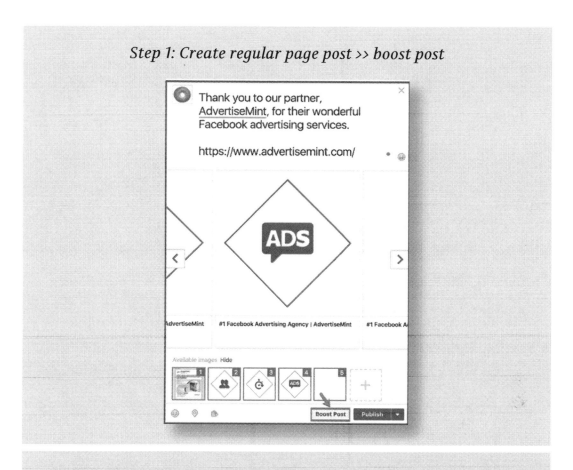

Step 2: Choose your target audience >> set a budget and duration

Step 3: Choose payment method >> click "Set Budget"

You can choose to pay with either your credit card or your PayPal account.

Step 4: Click "Publish"

The budget amount next to the publish button confirms that your post is a boosted post. As soon as you publish, your post will be sent to Facebook for review. Once approved, Facebook will show your post to your preferred audience.

Step 5: You're done

Your post will appear on your Facebook page's timeline. You can cancel the ad by deleting the post.

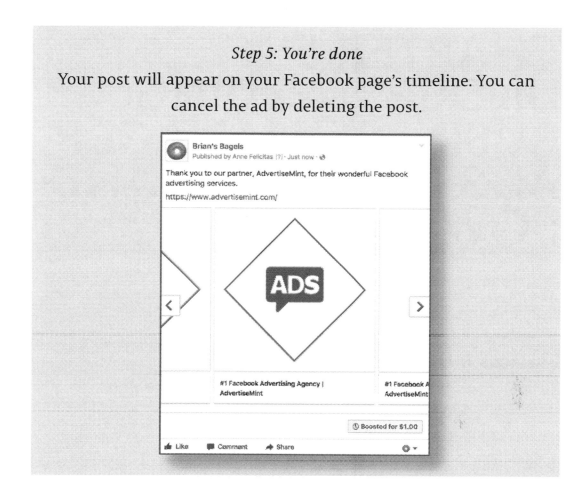

CHAPTER 5: UNDERSTANDING BUSINESS MANAGER, ADS MANAGER, AND POWER EDITOR

Business Manager

Business Manager is the website you use to manage all of your assets for Facebook advertising such as pages, ad accounts, Instagram accounts, product catalogs, and mobile apps. Business Manager allows you to easily access these assets in one place and grant access to those working with you. There are several features that are particularly important in Business Manager, features that I will discuss in this section.

Campaign Planner

How much should you spend on Facebook ads? Here's a tool that will help you answer that question. Campaign Planner, located in the Business Manager menu, is a tool that allows you to estimate the reach and frequency for a campaign based on the budget, ad placements, and target audience

Figure 5.1

Campaign planner in the Business Manager menu

you choose. After you create a plan for your campaigns, you can compare one campaign with the other and share campaign predictions with colleagues. In figure 5.2, I'm comparing a campaign with a $4,000 budget with a campaign with a $5,000 budget. The results show that the campaign with the $5,000 budget will have a higher reach and frequency than the campaign with the $4,000 budget.

Figure 5.2a A comparison of two campaigns

Figure 5.2b A comparison of two campaigns

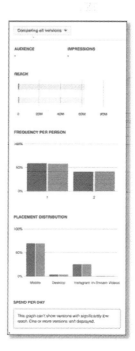

Figure 5.3
Campaign
planner charts

You can also analyze your results by viewing the chart on the right side of the screen (figure 5.3). In the chart, the analysis is broken down by frequency per person, placement distribution, and spend per day. To share the results, you can click the share button on the upper-right side of the screen. You can share your data through email or a shareable link. You can even download it as a CSV file.

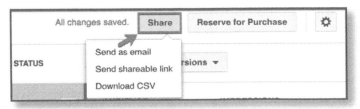

Figure 5.4 Various ways of sharing data

If you like the results you see, you can buy the plan by clicking "Reserve for Purchase" on the upper-right corner of your screen. The plan you create will automatically be saved. You can leave the screen and return to the plan at any time. However, be aware that if you wait too long to update your plan, it may become irrelevant. To make sure that yours is up to date, check the status of the plan that is represented in three different symbols: blue circle, gray circle, and red triangle. Blue circle means it's up to date; gray circle means it's not up to date; and red triangle means there's an error.

Figure 5.5 Reserving your plan for purchase

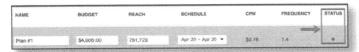

Figure 5.6 The blue circle indicates that the plan is up to date.

Automated Rules

If there's one thing I've learned in the past five years, it's that managing successful Facebook ad campaigns requires constant attention. There are many moving parts to your ad campaigns, and failure to monitor or manage your ads effectively is a surefire way to overpay Facebook for your ads. Facebook created automated rules to automate some of the most common tasks based on data from your campaigns, eliminating some of the time-consuming manual work by automatically applying rules to your ad campaigns. For example, you can create a rule to lower budgets and bids when CPAs are high or, conversely, to

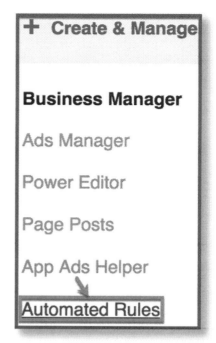

Figure 5.7
Where to find automated rules

raise them when CPAs are low. When you create an automated rule on Business Manager, you must choose an action, or the rule you want to apply when one or several conditions have been met, and a condition, or the circumstances in which Facebook must apply the rule you have chosen.

   Apply Rule To: Where you want the rule to apply. You can apply a rule to all active campaigns, ad sets, or ads.

   Action: What will happen when a condition has been met. Your options include turn off, send notification, adjust the budget, or adjust the manual bid.

Condition: This triggers the automated rule. You can select from a list of items such as daily spend, lifetime spend, frequency, results, and cost per result, just to name a few. You can then set the thresholds to greater than, is equal to, or is lesser than, and the number you wish. When a campaign, ad set, or ad reaches this threshold in the time range you select, the automated rule will complete the action you have chosen. The most common examples of automated rules are decreasing spend, stopping ads that are underperforming, and increasing the ad spend when an ad is performing well.

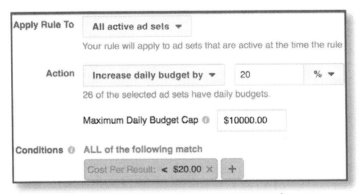

Figure 5.8 How to create a rule

Audience Insights

Most advertisers get wide-eyed when they discover the treasure trove of information made available by the audience insights tool, a tool that helps you understand your audience's interests and behaviors, enabling you to better target your ads. It shows you an exclusive report on demographics, lifestyles, interests, location, language, Facebook activity, behaviors, and purchase activity.

People often ask me where Facebook acquires all of its data. It comes from two sources: Facebook's users and third-party partners. Facebook acquires data from its users who voluntarily provide personal information upon registering for a Facebook account and developing their profiles. The information includes email, phone number, first and last names, address, relationship status, and job title. Facebook also acquires data from third-party partners such as Acxiom, Epsilon, Experian, Oracle Data Cloud, TransUnion, and WPP. Information these companies commonly provide include household income, home value, and purchasing behaviors. Facebook then links the email or phone number users listed on Facebook with the third-party partner's records.

It's important that you analyze your insights to better understand and target an audience. For example, if most of your audience is composed of women, you would then know to focus your targeting on women or to write copies that speak to women. Here's how to use audience insights.

Step 1: Business Manager tab >> "Plan" >> "Audience Insights"

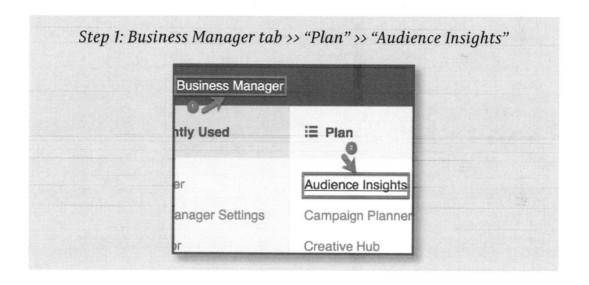

Step 2: Choose an audience

You will have three options: everyone on Facebook, people connected to your page, and custom audience.

Everyone on Facebook: If you choose this option, you will see insights on all Facebook users, even those who aren't in your customer list and who aren't connected to you via Facebook page or events. Choose this option if you want to understand data based on broad interests or taken from competitor pages.

People connected to your page: With this option you will see insights on people who have either liked or followed your page. Choose this option if you want to understand an existing audience.

Custom audience: With this option, you will see insights on customers from your customer list. Choose this option if you want to know more about an audience that is already using your brand.

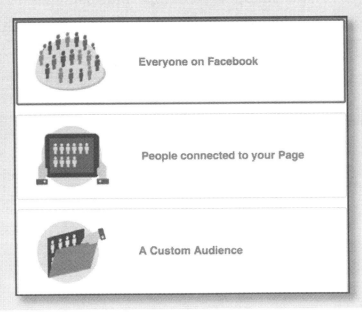

Step 3: Set your parameters

In this step, you must define the audience whose insights you want to see. You can choose the audience's country, age, gender, and interests.

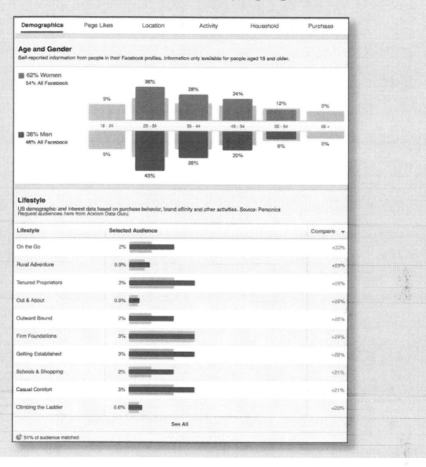

Step 4: Explore data

You can look at various parts of your demographics such age, gender, relationship status, job title, household information, and lifestyle.

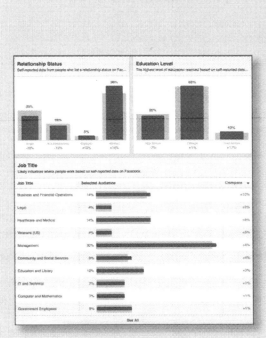

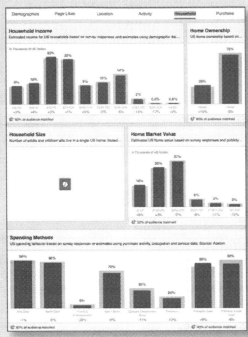

Delivery Insights

Delivery insights, which you can access while viewing ad sets in Ads Manager, is a tool that shows you problems with your ad's delivery. With this information, you can better diagnose delivery issues and improve results. The information in delivery insights also includes analyses explaining the reasons for delivery volatility and ways that you can address the problem. When accessing delivery insights, you will see three tabs that contain information about your ad set's performance.

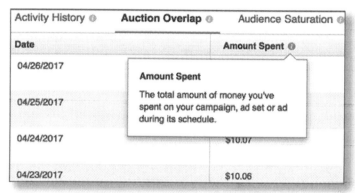

Figure 5.9 The three tabs of delivery insights

- **Activity:** This tab shows you the actions taken on a specific ad set, such as updates and deliveries.

- **Auction overlap:** An auction overlap, one of the causes of your ad set's poor performance, occurs when you target an overlapping audience, causing you to bid against yourself. In this tab, you'll gain access to information on other ad sets that overlap.

- **Audience saturation:** This situation occurs when an audience sees your ads multiple times and refuses to respond to them. The audience saturation tab will provide information on audience saturation, such as the percentage of your daily impressions that comes from people seeing your ad set for the first time.

You can access delivery insights in two ways:

· **Ads Manager:** Each ad set with a performance shift has a "See Delivery Insights" link.

· **A business notification:** When your ad set experiences a performance shift, Facebook will send you a notification that you can click to view. The notification will appear on the top-right corner of Ads Manager.

Only ad sets that have been running for at least five consecutive days, have at least 500 impressions, and have experienced a performance shift will have access to delivery insights.

Creative Hub

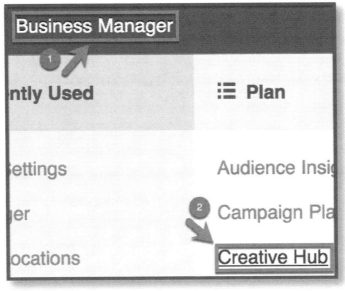

Figure 5.10 Where to find Creative Hub

Creative Hub is a website where advertisers can easily create, review, share, and test ad mockups. It focuses on mobile ads and explores the new ways advertisers can create attractive, compelling ads compressed within a mobile screen. Here's what you can do with Creative Hub:

- Browse through ad creatives designed by other brands and agencies at the Hub's inspiration gallery located under the "Get Inspired Tab." Featured ad formats include 360 videos, carousels, canvases, and single videos.

- Preview mockups in all available ad formats on Facebook and Instagram.

- Save mockups and return to them later.

- Collaborate and exchange ideas with your team. (This feature is only available to Business Manager account holders.)

- Generate a URL of your mockup to send to colleagues and clients.

- Check whether your image complies with Facebook's 20 percent text rule. (Text shouldn't take up 20 percent of the ad's image.)

App Ads Helper

If you have an app, then you should use Business Manager's app ads helper, a tool that troubleshoots and fixes any problems with your app. There are various app management actions you can do with this tool. You can verify your app, check your app's settings, install events, and view your app's history, installs, and bid type.

Ads Reporting

The ads reporting tool stores all of your saved reports. You can save your reports from the campaign, ad sets, or ads level in Ads Manager. Here are the steps to follow when you navigate through the ads reporting page.

Figure 5.11 Where to manage reports in ads reporting

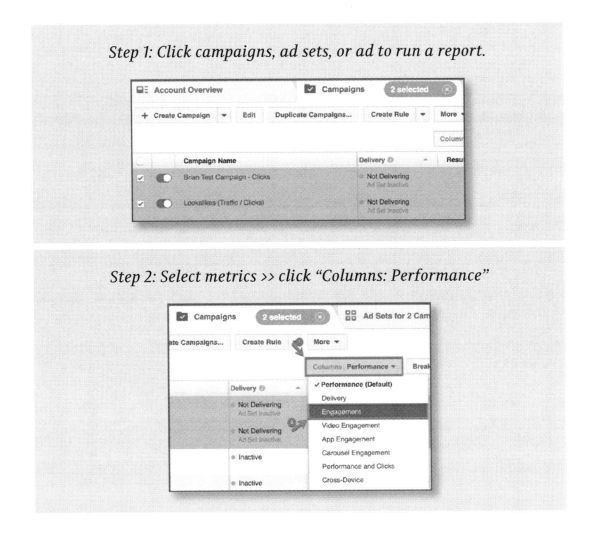

Step 1: Click campaigns, ad sets, or ad to run a report.

Step 2: Select metrics >> click "Columns: Performance"

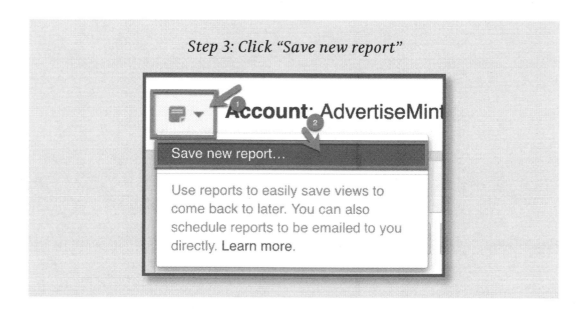

Step 3: Click "Save new report"

Custom Conversions

Custom conversions allow you to optimize and track for specific actions without adjusting your already existing pixel code, a process that requires replacing the pixels placed on the final page after the desired action is completed (e.g., order complete page). Although standard events are the preferred method of tracking because those fields appear first in the conversion tracking area, if you do not have a programmer on staff or if you are using an e-commerce platform such as Shopify, WooCommerce, or Magento, correctly implementing standard events can be a hassle, making custom conversions your best option. Custom conversions allow you to track a conversion event based on a URL string, which means you can enter in the URL of the page you want to mark as a conversion, and Facebook will track all the users who make it to that page. If you hate tinkering with code, you will love custom conversions because it is a more convenient way to optimize and track your customers' actions. Fortunately, setting up your custom conversions is fast and easy.

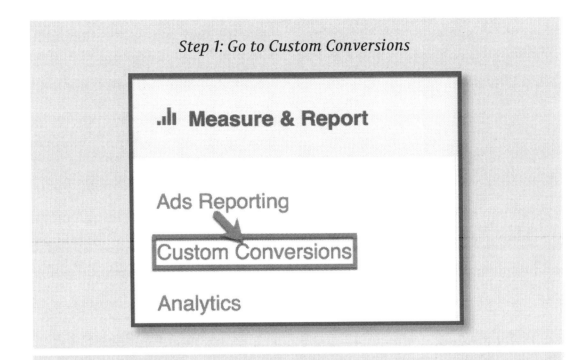

Step 1: Go to Custom Conversions

Step 2: Click "Create Custom Conversions"

Step 3: Create a custom conversion

Fill in the required information to create a custom conversion. By filling out these rules, you're helping Facebook determine whether a customer who visited your website converted.

1. Choose "**URL Contains**" and then type the URL keywords. By doing so, you're telling Facebook where you want the pixel to track in your website. In the example below, I used the keywords "/shoes" to tell the pixel that it should track customers who landed on my page with those keywords in the URL.

2. Choose a category. For mine, I chose "**Purchase.**" By choosing this, Facebook will track for purchases. After you have filled in the fields, click "**Next.**"

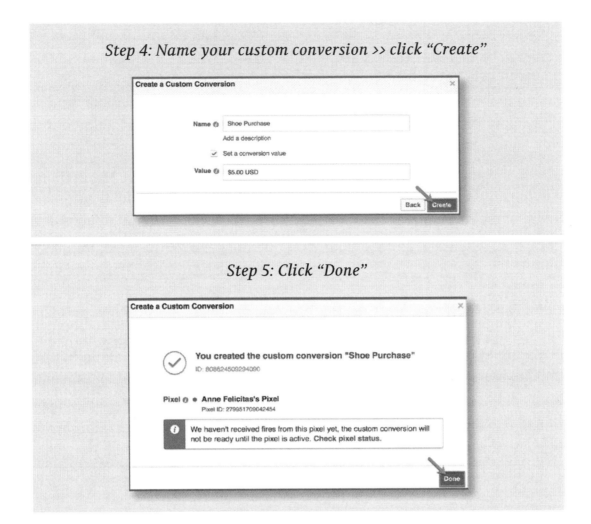

Images

When you visit the drop-down menu from Business Manager, you will see, under the assets section, an option labeled "Images." Clicking this will lead you to the images page, a page that contains all of the images you've ever uploaded for various ads. This page is a useful tool for revisiting past creatives.

Figure 5.11 Where to find images

Figure 5.12 A list of all the images uploaded to Business Manager

Pixels

Under the assets tab, you will also see an option labeled "Pixels." When you click that, you will be directed to a page that contains performance information about your pixel. From there, you will see a graph that displays when your pixel fired and a list that contains the URLs, domains, and devices your pixel fired from. On the upper-right side of the screen, you'll see important information about your pixel (pixel ID and code) that you will need when implementing your pixel to a website.

Figure 5.13 Where to find your pixels

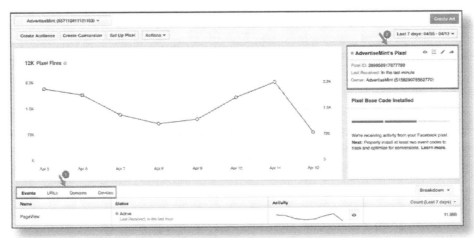

Figure 5.14 The pixel page

Offline Events

Offline Events is a tool that allows you to track offline conversions. Let's say you released an ad promoting your products. A customer, after seeing the ad every day for a week, decided to go to your nearest brick-and-mortar store to buy the product off the shelf. Although the customer didn't buy your product from your online store through your Facebook ad, the ad still influenced the customer's decision to purchase. Before Offline Events existed, you had no way of knowing whether your ad influenced a customer's offline purchase. To start tracking offline conversions, you need to create an Offline Event set where you can upload your data.

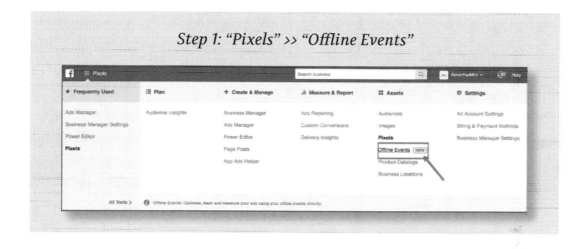

59

Step 2: Click "Create Offline Event Set"

Step 3: Name event set >> include description >> click "Create"

Step 4: Click "Upload Offline Events"

Step 5: Click "Next"

Step 6: Click "Upload"

Step 7: Click "Done"

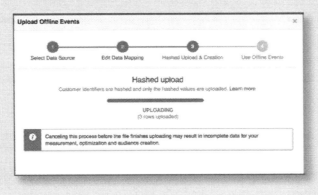

Step 8: Assign ad accounts to test offline event set (optional)

You can choose multiple accounts. Click "Next" or "Skip" to skip this step.

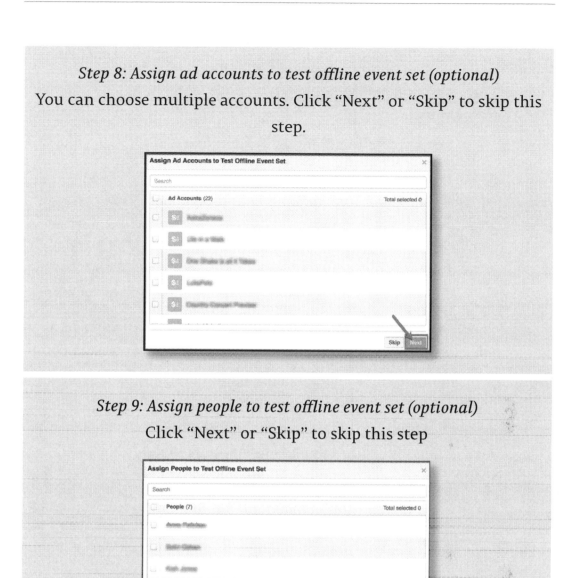

Step 9: Assign people to test offline event set (optional)

Click "Next" or "Skip" to skip this step

Product Catalogs

A product catalog contains a file called a product feed that has all of the products you want to advertise on Facebook. This list contains a description of each product, including an ID, name, category, availability, product URL, image URL, and other product attributes. You need product catalogs for dynamic product ads, ads that show products from your product catalog. If you want to upload a product catalog, you must go to the product catalogs page of Business Manager.

Step 1: Go to "Assets" >> "Product Catalogs"

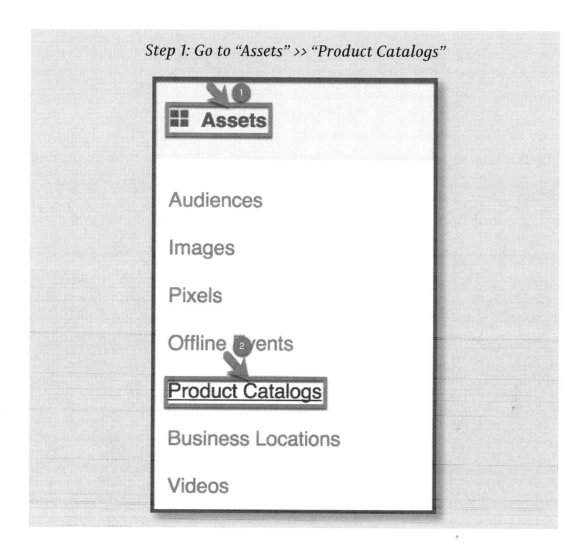

Step 2: Click "Create Catalog"

Step 3: Name your catalog >> select catalog type >> indicate owner of catalog

Step 4: Add product feed

Your product feed is a spreadsheet containing information about each of the products you want to advertise.

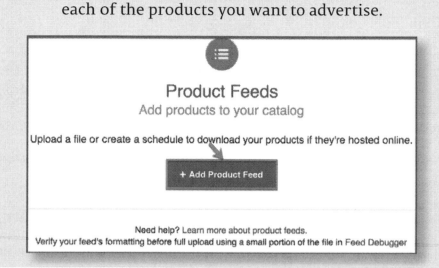

Step 5: Name your product feed >> choose currency >> select upload type

Step 6: Upload your product feed

Formats compatible for upload are CSV, TSV, RSS XML, and ATOM XML.

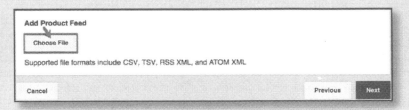

Step 7: Click "Next"

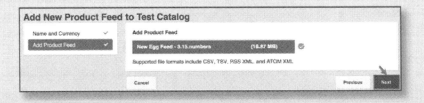

Step 8: You're done

An overview of your product catalog should appear.

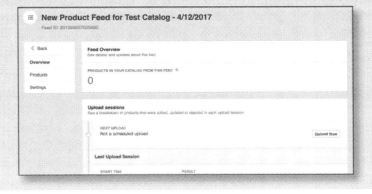

Business Locations

Your business might have multiple locations in multiple cities. If you were McDonald's, for instance, you would have 14,146 restaurants in the United States. Your multiple business locations pose one problem: how are you supposed to advertise for each of those 14,146 restaurants in one ad? This dilemma is particularly troubling for those who are trying to create ads with a store visits objective, an objective that sends people to your nearest business location. Fortunately, Facebook fixed this dilemma by creating the business locations feature, a feature that allows you to add multiple locations for a single business. After you do this, you can then dynamically show your customers information about your business locations in a single ad. To use the business locations feature for your store visits ad, you must first set up the main page of your business location.

Step 1: Go to "Assets" >> "Business Locations"

If you don't see business locations from the menu, it's likely because your ads have not been running for at least five consecutive days, do not have at least 500 impressions, and have not experienced a performance shift. When you've fulfilled those three requirements, the tool will appear.

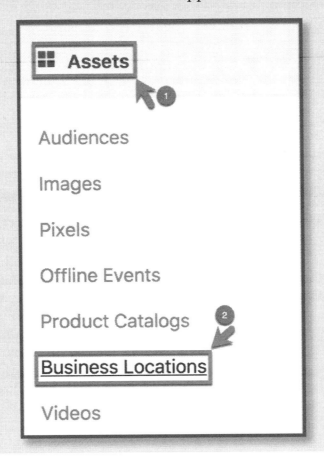

Step 2: Set up main page

To set up business locations, you must first set up a main page. A main page functions more like a branding page than a business page. Whereas a business page contains your business's address, reviews, and ratings, a branding page does not because it represents your business as a brand rather than a specific brick-and-mortar store. If you choose a business page to be your main page, the address, reviews, and ratings shown in the page will disappear. This happens because your business page will be converted to a brand page. To avoid this, either use your already existing brand page (not the business page) as the main page or create a new one. Then click "**Set Main Page**" to choose your main page.

Click the page you want to set as your main page. If you can't find your page from the drop-down menu, you can contact Facebook support and ask the support team to set up Business Locations for you.[8] They will respond to you within twenty-four hours, and they will be able to set up your business location's main page within two to three business days.

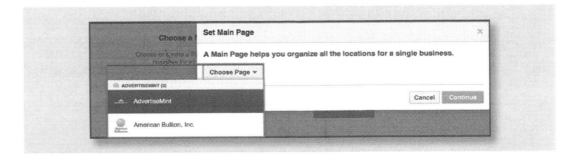

Step 3: Add Locations

You have three options: upload a file containing all of your business locations (this is highly recommended for businesses with hundreds or thousands of locations), set a location from an already existing business page, or add a single location (a great option for businesses with only a handful of locations). After you've added all of your business locations, the locations will appear in the page.

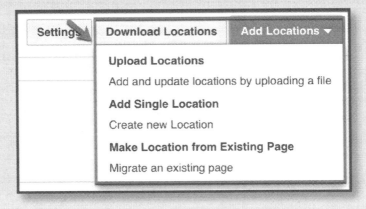

Ad Account Settings

Ad account settings is the place where you can view and update ad account settings and edit your account information, such as your account name, the country your business is in, and your business's address. On this page, you can also edit your notification settings (as shown in figure 5.16). For instance, you can choose to disable notifications about product updates, ad approval, or ad review decisions. As figure 5.17 illustrates, you can also view, add, or remove ad account roles. If you want to view your settings for a different ad, simply click the drop-down menu on the upper-left corner of your screen (see figure 5.18 for an example).

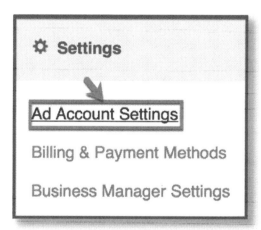

Figure 5.15 Where to find ad account settings

Figure 5.16 A look inside the ad account settings page

Figure 5.17 Viewing, adding, or removing ad accounts

Figure 5.18 A dropdown menu containing other ad accounts

Business Manager Settings

If you want to view or change your Business Manager settings, you must visit the Business Manager settings page, which is accessible from two different areas: the upper-right corner of your screen and Business Manager's drop-down menu under the settings section.

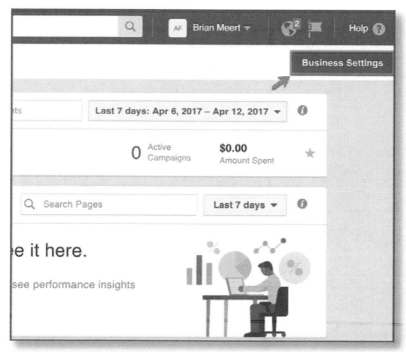

Figure 5.19 The business settings button on the main page

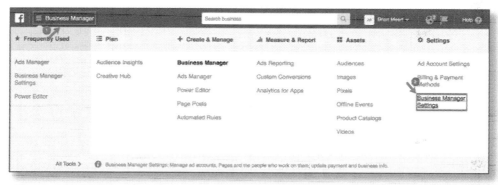

Figure 5.20 The business settings in the Business Manager menu

You can do numerous tasks within Business Manager settings. You can view and manage people and assets such as ad accounts, apps, pixels, product catalogs, Instagram accounts, block lists, offline event sets, shared audiences, and source groups. You can also add your payment method, edit your business information, set preferences, and manage requests.

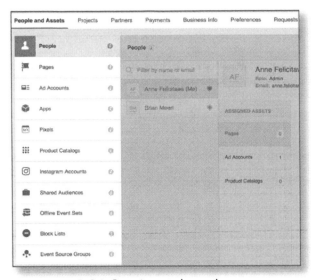

Figure 5.21 Settings dropdown menu

Ads Manager

Ads Manager, accessible from Business Manager's drop-down menu, is a dashboard within Business Manager where you can create, view, and edit ads as well as access performance reports for all of your campaigns. You can also view all of your Facebook payment history, change your bids and budgets, export ad performance reports from the reports tab, and pause or restart your ads at any time. Ads Manager contains features that will help you better manage your ads. Those features include data exports, filters, and performance views, just to name a few.

Figure 5.22 Where to find Ads Manager

Your Accounts

You can view all of your ad accounts on Ads Manager and easily switch from one to the other. You will also find your ad account number there, which you will need when requesting ad account help from Facebook or when working with a partner who needs access to one or all of your accounts.

Figure 5.23 A dropdown menu containing ad accounts

Create Ad Button

If you want to create an ad, you can do so by clicking the create ad button.

Figure 5.24 The create-ad button

Search

Below the create ad button, you will find the search tab, which you will use to search a campaign name, ad set name, ad name, and campaign ID, among many others.

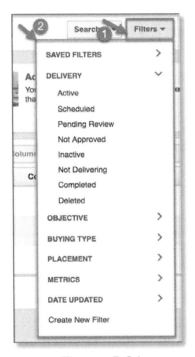

Figure 5.25
Search by name or ID

Filter Options

Next to the search button, you will find the filters button. With this, you can filter what you want to see on your ads report. For example, if you want to know which of your ads are delivering, you can choose to filter by active ads. You can also filter by objective, buying type, and metrics.

Filter by Days

You can also choose which campaigns you want to view by days. For instance, if you want to see campaigns from the last seven, fourteen, or thirty days, you can do so by clicking the respective tab.

Figure 5.26
Filter options

Figure 5.27 The last-30-days tab

Save Your Report

If you want to save your campaign report, you can do so by clicking the icon that looks like a document next to your account name.

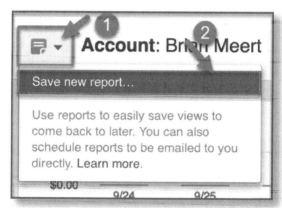

Figure 5.28 Saving your report

View Your Performance

If you want to know how your campaigns are doing, you can do so by clicking the columns tab. You can choose specific performances you want to view such as delivery, engagement, video engagement, and app engagement, among many others.

Figure 5.29 Viewing campaign performance

Breakdown

Next to the performance tab, you will see a breakdown tab. This tab shows you the breakdowns of your campaigns. If you want a report of your audience's age in your campaigns, you can filter by age. If you want to see other data for gender, country, region, or impression device, among many others, you can also find that in the breakdown dropdown menu.

Figure 5.30 The breakdown tab

Export Data

If you want to download this data for your own records, you can do so by exporting the files into a spreadsheet.

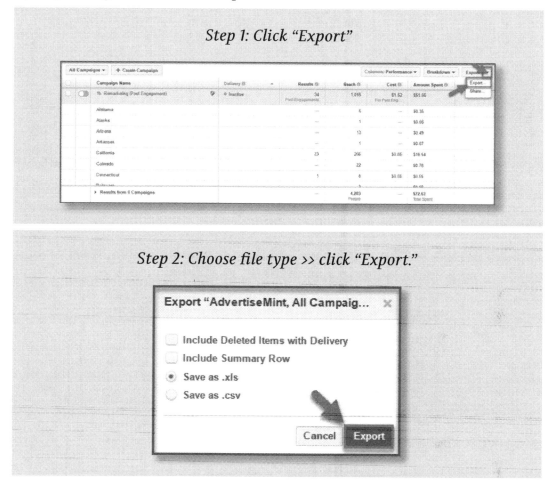

Step 1: Click "Export"

Step 2: Choose file type >> click "Export."

Step 3: Download file

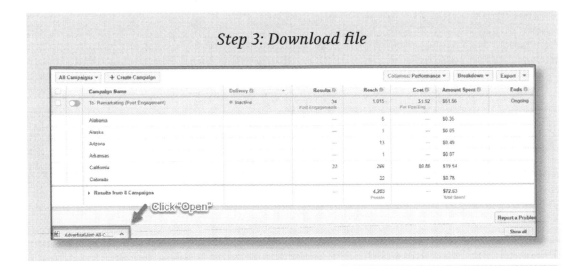

Step 4: You're done

Your file has been saved according to your chosen file type.

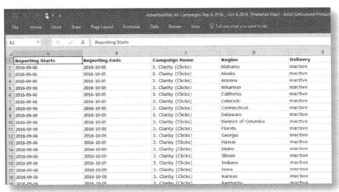

Figure 5.31 Image of a file type

Ads Manager Mobile App

Fortunately, you can keep a close eye on your account even when you're away from your computer. After recognizing the growing number of advertisers who use their phones more often than their computers, Facebook launched the Ads Manager app in 2015, available for iOS, Android phones, and tablets. The app helps you manage and monitor your accounts while on the go and allows you to track performance, create and edit ads, ad budgets and schedules, receive push notifications, pause or resume campaigns, and respond to alerts. There are four features that make managing your accounts easier while on the go: the home page, comparative view of your campaigns, weekly summary, and recommended actions.

Home page: The home page contains quick-view summaries of your accounts, ads, and pages.

Campaigns: You can view several campaigns side by side to compare their metrics.

Weekly summary: The app also provides a weekly summary of your campaign performances as well as other information about your ad account and creatives.

Recommended actions: The app will also recommend actions to help you improve your ad performance.

The Ads Manager app allows you to access your accounts anywhere, whether you're sunbathing by the pool, sipping piña coladas in Mexico, or sitting in the midnight train going anywhere.

Power Editor

Power Editor, a dashboard designed for advertisers who create and manage multiple ads at once, allows you to do advanced tasks such as importing data from Excel and managing bulk ads, individual ads, and ads sets.

Figure 5.32 Power Editor in the Business Manager tab

In Power Editor, you can edit ads from the campaign, ads set, or ads level. Think of these levels as a matryoshka doll. Open the campaign level, and you will find ad sets within it. Open the ad sets level, and you will find ads within it. Open the ads level, and you will find a single ad within it. The deeper you go into these levels, the smaller they get. The ads you create are automatically organized in these three levels. If you want to view or edit certain parts of your ads, you must visit certain levels. For instance, you can edit your audience in the ads level and your objective in the campaign level. As you probably have guessed, you can do different things in different levels.

Figure 5.33 The three editing levels in Power Editor

Campaign level: In the campaign level, which contains one or more ad sets and ads, you can choose an objective, turn on or off all ad sets and ads, and measure the performance of each objective across multiple ad sets and ads.

Ad sets level: In the ad sets level, which contains one or more ads, you can choose your audience, schedule, budget, and placements. You can do three things that you can't do in other levels: you can create separate ad sets for each audience, choose either a daily budget or a lifetime budget, and test ad sets against each other.

Ads level: In the ads level, which contains only a single ad, you can add creatives, copies, and links.

It's important that you understand these levels to easily improve your ad's performance. Understanding the structure helps you measure results, test different audiences, and identify which ads work best.

CHAPTER 6:
AD ACCOUNT SETUP

At this point, you have enough knowledge of Business Manager to know how to navigate its platform. You know the features within Ads Manager and Power Editor, and you know how to use them. The next step is to teach you how to set up your ad account for advertising, a process that I follow when I get my clients started with Facebook ads.

Connecting with Your Partner

The first thing I do with my new clients is ask them to give me access to their ad accounts so that I can advertise on behalf of their business. In this section, I'll teach you how to connect with your partner.

Sharing Agency Access with an Ad Account

To connect with your partner, you must first find your ad account ID, which you can retrieve from the accounts tab in Ads Manager. Each account name on the drop-down menu will show an account ID. Once you've copy and pasted, wrote down, or memorized your account ID, you can send it to your client, who will then use it to add you as a partner. There are two ways you can connect with a partner: you can request access (via a business ID or by sending a link) or claim your partner's ad account.

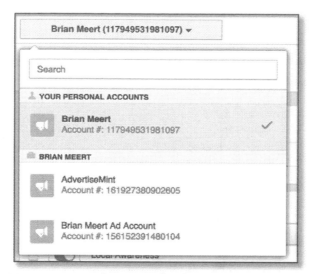

Figure 6.1 Where to find your account ID

Option 1: Request access using business ID

Step 2: Click "Ad Accounts"

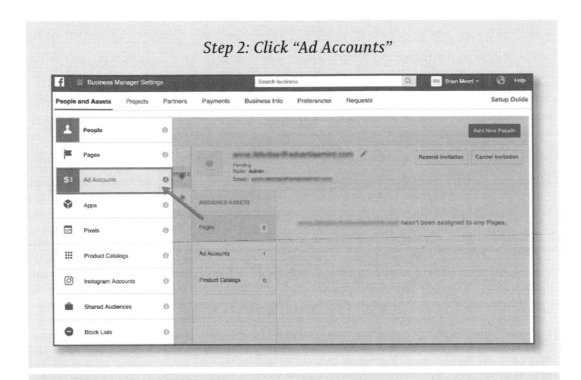

Step 3: Choose ad account >> click "Assign Partner"

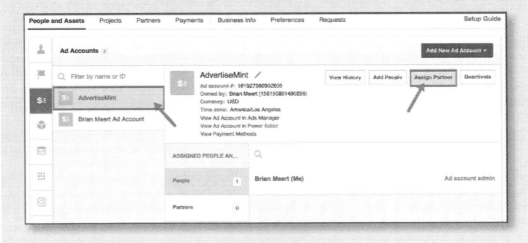

Step 4: Assign ad account using partner's business ID >> choose role >> connect

Admin: Admins have full access to ad accounts and pages. They can create and modify ad campaigns, assign roles, change settings, and more.

Advertiser: Although advertisers don't have full access to ad accounts, they can make advertising-related actions such as editing billing information and editing and creating ads.

Analyst: Analysts can review the performance of your campaigns but cannot edit or modify them.

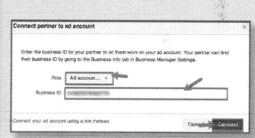

Step 5: Click "Done"

Your partner will receive an alert about the access to the account.

Option 2: Send link

Step 1: Select role

In the first option, you chose to assign an ad account using a business ID. In this option, you will send a link instead of using a business ID. Click "**Select a role**" then click "**Ad account admin**" on the drop-down menu. 1: Go to settings

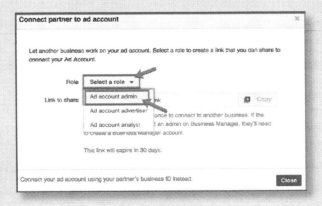

Step 2: Click copy >> close

Copy and send the copied link to your partner.

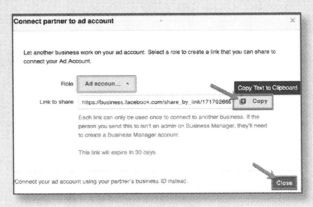

Option 3: Claiming an Ad Account

Claiming an ad account differs from requesting access. When you claim an ad account, you're claiming complete ownership of that account— you're claiming that it's yours. People who claim ad accounts normally claim an ad account that they created, not an account that someone else created. When you request access, on the other hand, you're not taking the account away from the owner. You're simply asking for access so you and the owner can work together on campaigns. If you're an agency or if you're advertising on behalf of the account owner, you should request access instead. Nonetheless, it's important to learn how to claim an ad account in the event that you need to do so.

Step 1: Go to "Business Settings" >> "People and Assets" >> "Ad Accounts" >> "Add New Ad Accounts >> "Add an Ad Account"

Step 2: Enter ad account ID >> click "Add Ad Account"

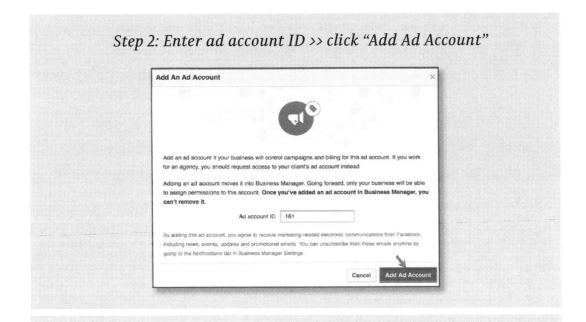

Step 3: Click "OK"

Once you've submitted your request, you will have to wait for the admin's approval.

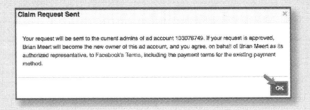

Creating a New Ad Account

Although this rarely happens, there might come a time when you will have to create a new ad account (perhaps your ad account was blocked by Facebook or labeled as spam by users). You can add a new ad account in the ad account section of Business Settings.

Step 1: Click "Add New Ad Accounts" >> "Create a New Ad Account"

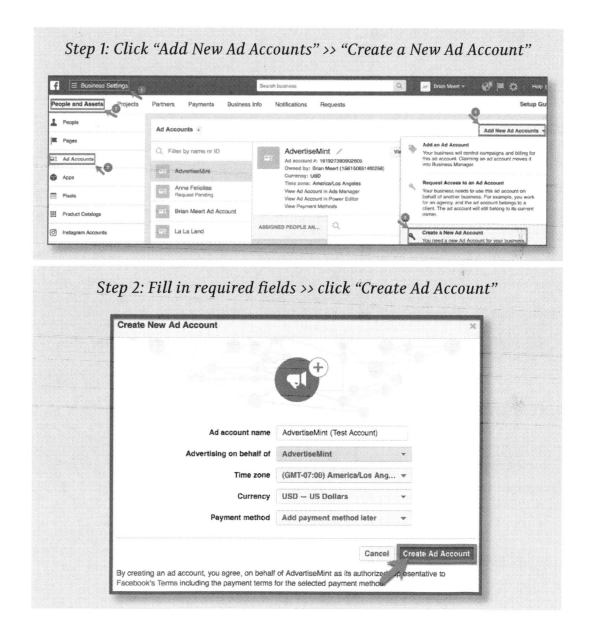

Step 2: Fill in required fields >> click "Create Ad Account"

Step 3: Add people to your account

You can assign roles while selecting people. Because this step is optional, you can choose to skip it. Otherwise, choose who you want to have access and then click "**Save Changes**."

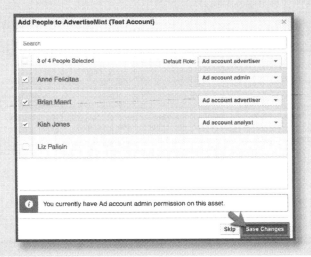

Step 4: Click "OK"

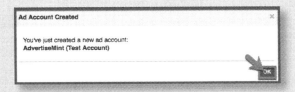

Step 5: You're done

Granting Permissions to Ad Accounts and Pages

Often, managing accounts and pages by your lonesome is a difficult endeavor. With a business to run and a personal life to maintain, overseeing multiple assets can be overwhelming and exhausting. Fortunately, adding people on Business Manager to lend you some extra help is fast and easy. On Business Manager, you can add multiple people to your ad accounts and pages and assign them roles.

Assigning Ad Account Roles

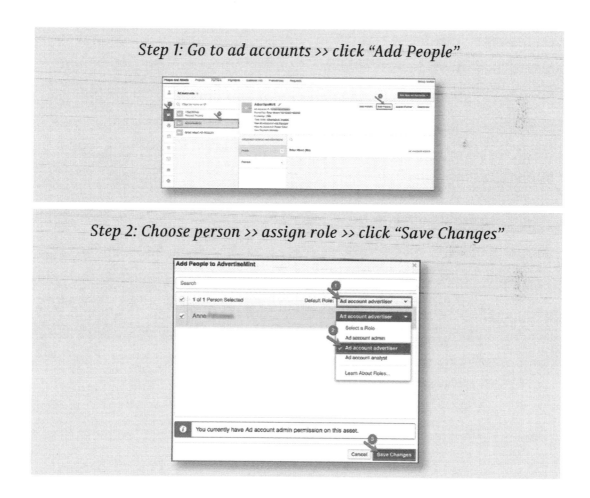

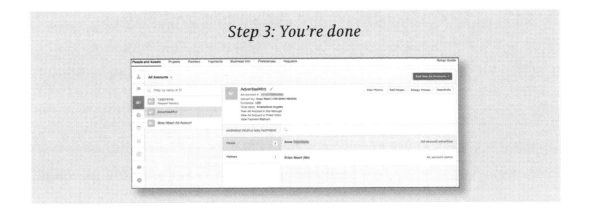

Step 3: You're done

Assigning Page Roles

Let's say you want other people, your employees perhaps, to help you manage your Facebook page. In order for people to co-manage a page, they must first receive page permissions from you. However, in order for you to assign page roles, you must first have a Facebook page claimed in Business Manager. If you don't have a Facebook page claimed, start from step one. If you already have a Facebook page claimed, skip to step five. 7

Step 1: Go to people and assets >> click "Add New Pages" >> "Add a Page"

Step 2: Click "Claim Page"

To claim a page, you must already be an admin of that page. Search for your page by either entering your Facebook page's name or its URL. After claiming a page, click "**Claim Page**."

Step 3: Click "OK"

Step 4: Click "Add People"

Here, you will be able to assign roles.

Step 5: Choose person >> select role >> click "Save Changes"

Step 6: You're done

Setting Up Your Facebook Pixel

The next step in setting up your ad account is to set up your Facebook pixel, a piece of JavaScript code that allows you to measure, optimize, and build an audience for your campaign. With the pixel, you can track conversions, create a lookalike audience based on those who converted (only after the pixel has tracked a minimum of one hundred conversions), and market to those who converted.

There are three main benefits of using the pixel. First, you can use the pixel's data to create a custom audience. Second, you can use the custom audience data, which provides never-before-seen information on website visitors' demographics, interests, and purchase behaviors, as a secondary resource to Google Analytics or other analytics services. Third, you can use the pixel's data to remarket to visitors who have visited specific pages of your site using dynamic product ads. For example, you can show couch-related ads only to those who have viewed couches on your website or show ads that remind those who abandoned their carts to finalize their purchase.

Because I don't want you to make the mistake of running ads without pixel tracking, I'm encouraging you to create one before creating your ads. You can create a Facebook pixel under the assets section of Business Manager.

Creating, Installing, Sharing, and Editing Your Pixel

In this section you will learn how to create, install, share, and edit your pixel.

Creating a Pixel

After creating your pixel, you will need to install it into your website so that the pixel will track web visitors.

Installing Pixel

Step 1: Click "Install Pixel Now"

Step 2: Copy Code

Copy the code and paste it between the headers (<head> </head>) of your website. Once pasted between the headers, the pixel will track web visits on every page of your website.

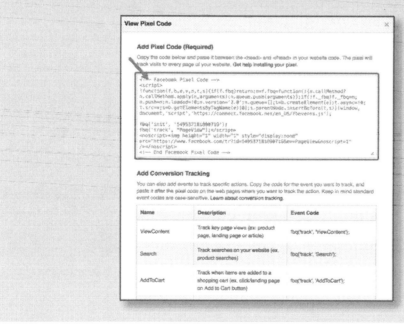

Sharing the Pixel

If you want to send your pixel code to your web developer, you can do so via email.

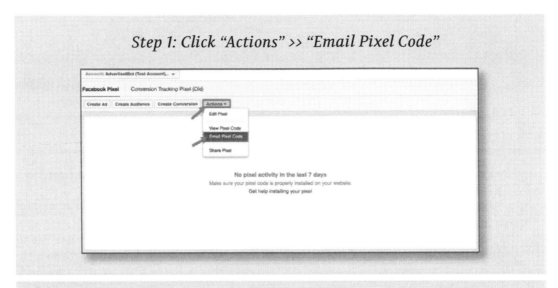

Step 1: Click "Actions" >> "Email Pixel Code"

Step 2: Type recipient's email >> click "Send"

Step 3: Click "Done"

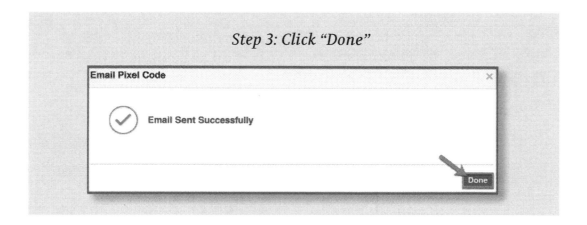

You can also share your pixel with a partner using an account ID.

Step 1: Click "Actions" >> "Share Pixel"

Step 2: Click "Go to Business Manager"

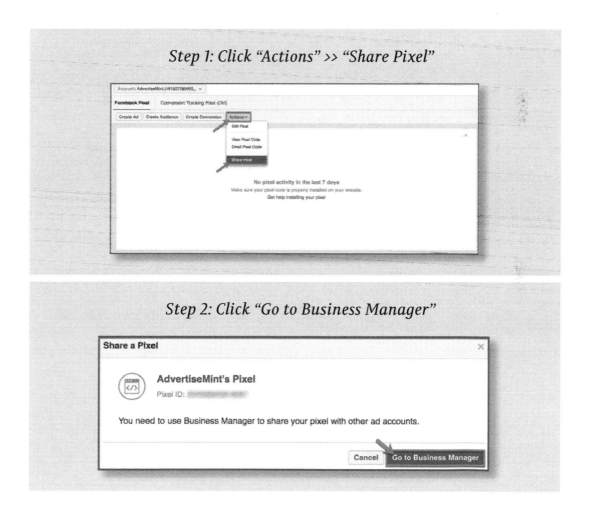

Step 3: Click "Assign Partner"

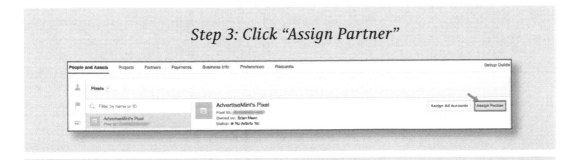

Step 4: Enter partner's account ID >> click "Confirm"

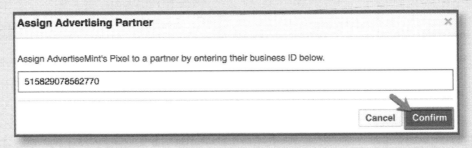

Step 5: You're done

The name of the partner with whom you shared your pixel should appear in the pixels section of Business Settings.

Editing a Facebook Pixel

If you want to change your pixel's name or if you spot an embarrassing typo you want to correct, you can edit your pixel at any time.

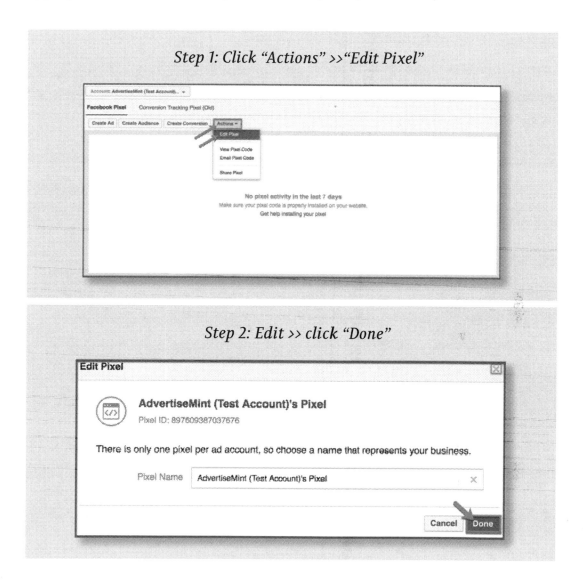

Step 1: Click "Actions" >>"Edit Pixel"

Step 2: Edit >> click "Done"

Installing Pixels to Websites

Although earlier I said that you must install your pixel between the headers of your website, that may not always be the case because different websites require you to place your pixel in different areas. This section will show you how to install your pixel in the six most commonly used websites: WordPress, Google Tag Manager, Shopify, Squarespace, BigCommerce, and Wix.

WordPress

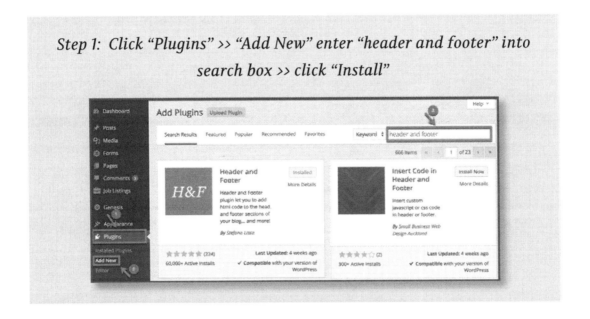

Step 1: Click "Plugins" >> "Add New" enter "header and footer" into search box >> click "Install"

Step 2: Go to "Settings" >> "Header and Footer" >> "Page header and footer" >> paste pixel into the box >> save

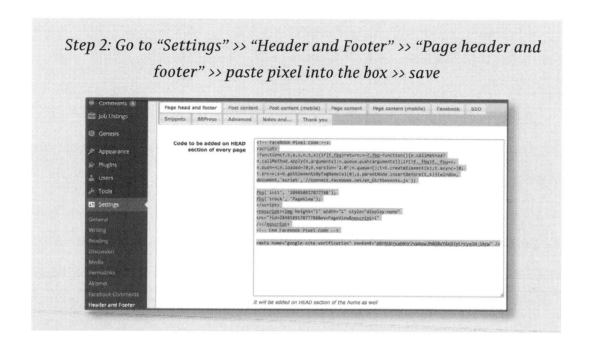

Google Tag Manager

Step 1: Go to "Workspace" >> "New Tag"

Step 2: Go to "Tag Configuration" >> "Choose a tag type to begin setup"

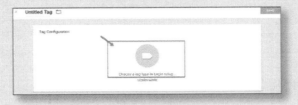

Step 3: Scroll to "Custom" >> click "Custom HTML"

Step 4: Paste your pixel code under "HTML"

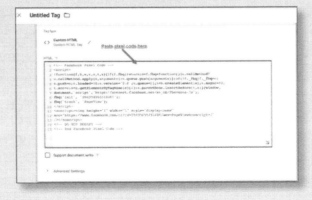

Step 5: Scroll to "Triggering" >> click "Choose a trigger to make this tag fire"

Step 6: Click "All Pages"

Step 7: Click "Save"

Step 8: Name tag >> save

Step 9: You're done

All changes should appear under "Workspace Changes." Once you're finished, click "Publish" to publish your changes.

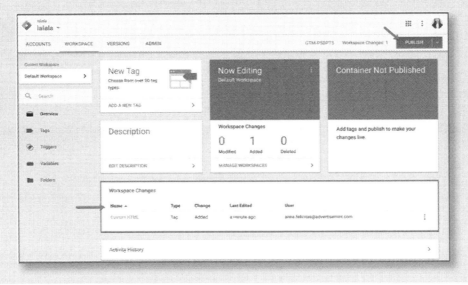

Shopify

Step 1: Find Your Pixel ID

From your pixel code, copy your pixel ID, the highlighted number indicated below.

Step 2: Go to Shopify >> "Online Store" >> "Facebook Pixel" >> paste your pixel ID

Step 3: Save pixel

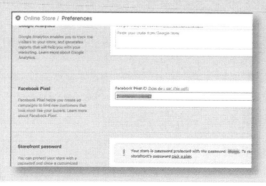

Squarespace

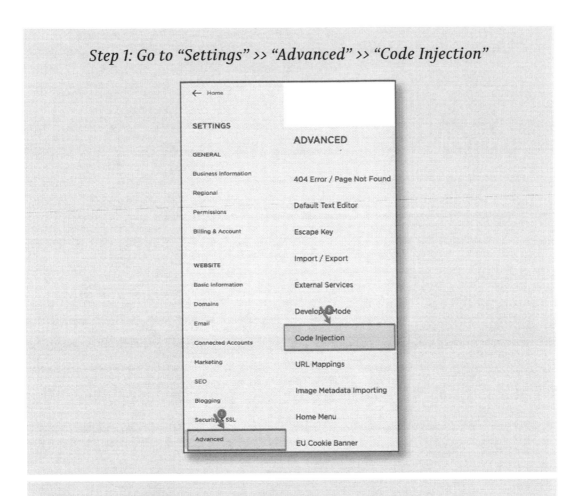

Step 1: Go to "Settings" >> "Advanced" >> "Code Injection"

Step 2: Paste pixel code into header >> save

BigCommerce: BluePrint Theme

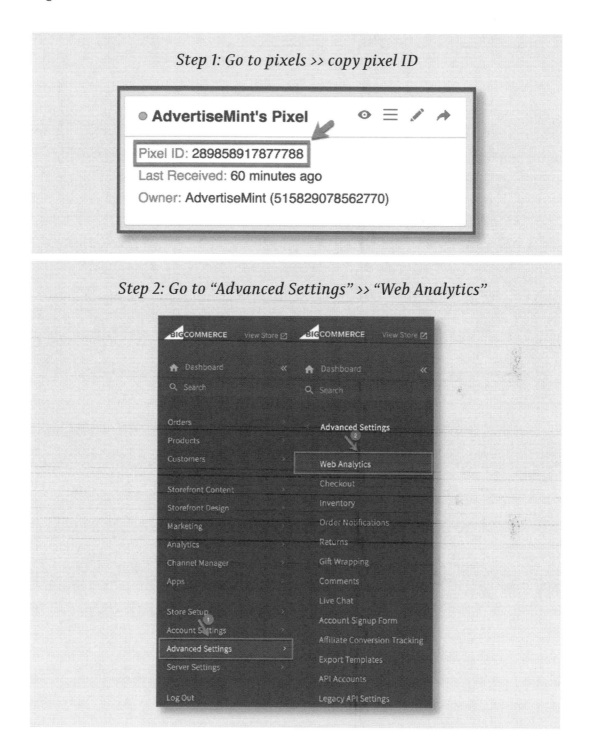

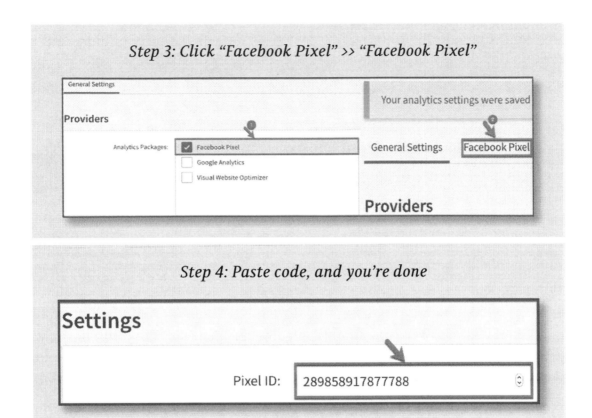

Step 3: Click "Facebook Pixel" >> "Facebook Pixel"

Step 4: Paste code, and you're done

BigCommerce: Stencil Theme

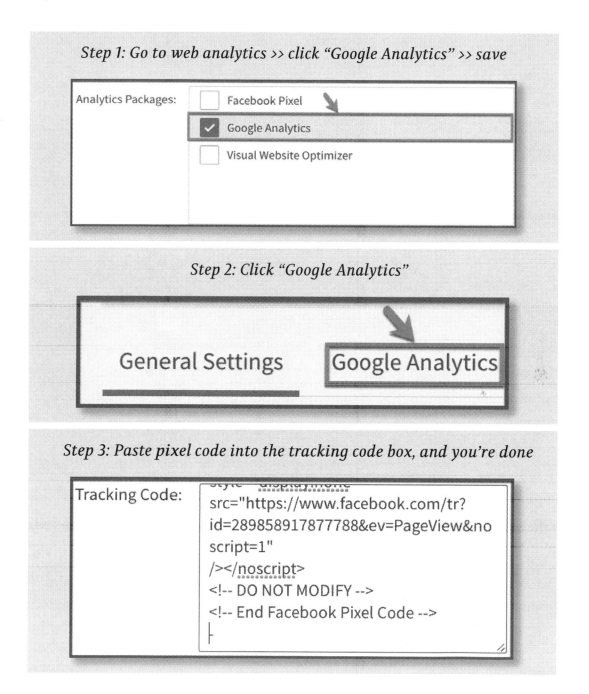

Step 1: Go to web analytics >> click "Google Analytics" >> save

Analytics Packages:

☐ Facebook Pixel

☑ Google Analytics

☐ Visual Website Optimizer

Step 2: Click "Google Analytics"

General Settings   Google Analytics

Step 3: Paste pixel code into the tracking code box, and you're done

Tracking Code:

```
src="https://www.facebook.com/tr?
id=289858917877788&ev=PageView&no
script=1"
/></noscript>
<!-- DO NOT MODIFY -->
<!-- End Facebook Pixel Code -->
```

Wix

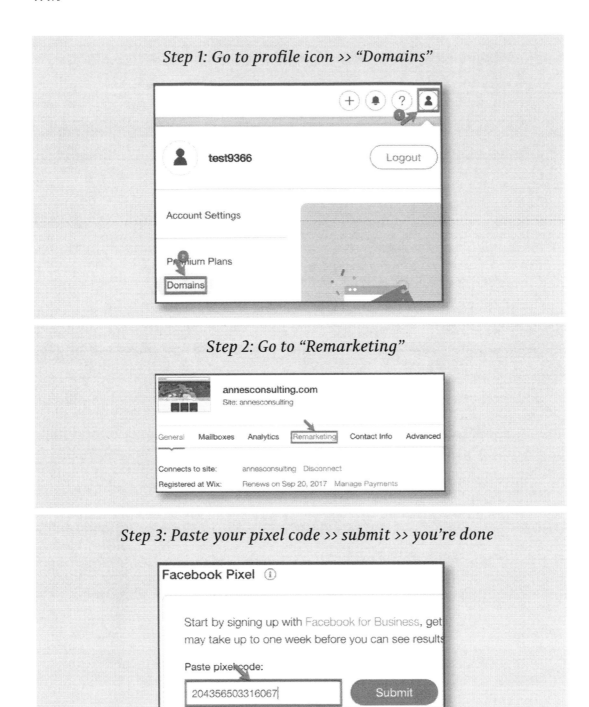

Troubleshooting Your Pixel

One valuable tool that you certainly must download is the Facebook Pixel Helper, a Chrome extension that validates your Facebook pixel, checks that it works properly, troubleshoots errors, and improves its performance. I use this tool to ensure that my clients' pixels are firing properly to elude disastrous results. Because a misfiring pixel will fail to track web visitors, you, with no data to upload, will be unable to create a new custom audience of interested buyers to whom you can retarget ads. I cannot stress this enough—the Facebook pixel is an essential part of your campaign. (You will see the pixel's important role resurface in this book.) Even more, a *working* Facebook pixel is an essential part of your campaign.

You can download the Pixel Helper or free from Google Chrome's web store. Once downloaded, the Pixel Helper icon, represented by the symbol </>, will appear on the upper-right hand corner of your browser.

Downloading the Facebook Pixel Helper

Step 1: Go to Google Chrome store >> "Add to Chrome"

Step 2: Click "Add extension"

Step 3: You're done

Your pixel helper should be located on the upper-right corner of your tool bar. Click it to activate.

To test whether the pixels on your site are working, check whether the Pixel Helper icon is green, yellow, gray, or red.

Green: Your pixel is firing correctly.
Yellow: Your pixel is firing, but there's an error.
Red: Your pixel is not firing.
Gray: You don't have a pixel installed.

If your Pixel Helper is green—great. You have nothing to worry about. All of your pixels are firing correctly. Often, you will see a green number displayed on the icon. Don't be alarmed. That number indicates the number of pixels found on your web page.

If your helper is glowing yellow or red, you have some problems to fix. There are a few reasons why your pixel isn't working correctly. One reason is you installed the pixel for a purchase event, but you didn't have a product catalog synced, causing your Pixel Helper to turn yellow. A yellow status means your pixel is still firing and collecting data, but there is something wrong with how a certain piece of information from your website is syncing with Facebook.

Another reason is simply this: your pixel was not installed correctly. If this is your problem, your Pixel Helper will glow red. If you don't immediately fix an incorrectly installed pixel, three things can happen: one, no data transfers to Facebook; two, the pixel will be unable to track all users visiting your website; and three, tracking will be duplicated, completely spoiling your data. If you click the pixel icon, you will see the information for debugging your pixel and the data tracked by your pixel.

People who have multiple pixels installed in their websites will often experience pixel problems. Although it's possible to have fully functioning multiple pixels on your site, problems may occur when all of your pixels have not loaded before your website fully loaded. It's vital each pixel loads before your website does.

Figure 6.2 A pixel helper installed to your web browser

Custom Conversions and Standard Events

As I previously mentioned, the Facebook pixel tracks customers' actions on your website. However, if you want to track people's actions on each page of your website, you must let your pixel know which pages you want it to track. For example, if you only wanted to know who added products to his or her cart, you will likely want to track the add-to-cart page. You can track certain actions on certain pages of your website using two tools: custom conversions and standard events.

Custom conversions, which is easier to set up than standard events, allows you to optimize and track for specific actions without making adjustments to your already existing pixel code by replacing the pixels placed on individual success pages. Custom conversions, then, does not work the same as standard events. Unlike custom conversions, with standard events, you will need to alter the Facebook pixel on specific pages.

Creating Custom Conversions

Step 1: Go to custom conversions >> click "Create Custom Conversions"

Step 2: Create a Custom Conversion

Afterward, fill in the required information to create a custom conversion. By filling out these rules, you are helping Facebook determine whether a customer who visited your website converted. Choose "**URL Contains**" and then type the URL keywords. By doing so, you are telling Facebook where in your website you want it to track. In the example below, I used "**/**shoes" to tell Facebook I want to track customers who landed on my page with these keywords on the URL. Then choose a category. For mine, I chose "**Purchase.**" By choosing this, Facebook will track for purchases. After you filled in the fields, click "**Next.**"

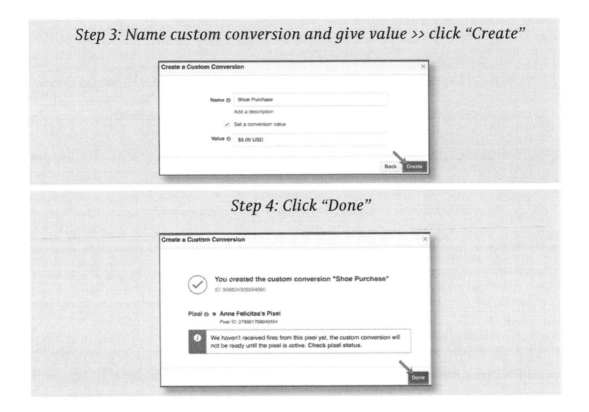

Step 3: Name custom conversion and give value >> click "Create"

Step 4: Click "Done"

As illustrated, tracking actions using custom conversions only takes a few steps. Standard events, however, is not as easy because you would need to modify every pixel code on all the web pages you want to track. If you are not code savvy, and you feel apprehensive about editing your website's code, then you should use custom conversions instead. Otherwise, standard events is highly recommended because it's more accurate, and it gives you more features. For example, if you wanted to track a thank-you page and selected the keywords "thank you" for the URL rule in custom conversions, your custom conversions may accidentally include other URLs with the thank-you keywords that are not thank-you pages. With standard events, however, there will be less room for error because you will place the code on the exact page that you want to track.

Standard events is essential to tracking users through critical funnels. It allows you to see users who viewed a specific product, added it to their cart, initiated checkout, and purchased. With standard events correctly installed, you can display ads to people who have added something to their carts but then abandoned for whatever reason. With standard events, you can track nine actions using their corresponding codes. You must place these codes before the closing script of the Facebook pixel's base code. Adding in the standard event code will indicate to the pixel that that is the specific type of event you want to track.

Website action	Standard event code
View content	fbq('track', 'ViewContent');
Search	fbq('track', 'Search');
Add to cart	fbq('track', 'AddToCart');
Add to wish list	fbq('track', 'AddToWishlist');
Initiate checkout	fbq('track', 'InitiateCheckout');
Add payment info	fbq('track', 'AddPaymentInfo');
Make purchase	fbq('track', 'Purchase', {value: '0.00', currency: 'USD'});
Lead	fbq('track', 'Lead');
Complete registration	fbq('track', 'CompleteRegistration');

Figure 6.3 Standard event codes

```
<!-- Facebook Pixel Code -->
<script>
!function(f,b,e,v,n,t,s){if(f.fbq)return;n=f.fbq=function(){n.callMethod?
n.callMethod.apply(n,arguments):n.queue.push(arguments)};if(!f._fbq)f._fbq=n;
n.push=n;n.loaded=!0;n.version='2.0';n.queue=[];t=b.createElement(e);t.async=!0;
t.src=v;s=b.getElementsByTagName(e)[0];s.parentNode.insertBefore(t,s)}(window,
document,'script','//connect.facebook.net/en_US/fbevents.js');

fbq('init', '1234567890');
fbq('track', "PageView");

fbq('track', 'Purchase', {value: '0.00', currency: 'USD'});

</script>
<noscript><img height="1" width="1" style="display:none"
src="https://www.facebook.com/tr?id=1234567890&ev=PageView&noscript=1"
/></noscript>
<!-- End Facebook Pixel Code -->
```

Figure 6.4 Example of a standard event code in a pixel

CHAPTER 7: CREATING FACEBOOK ADS

I don't mean to show a lack of confidence, but creating your first Facebook ad will be difficult and confusing. Before I became the CEO of my company, I was just like you. Completely new to Facebook advertising, I was both amazed by its potential and frustrated by its user unfriendliness. Although uploading ads has always been straightforward to me (pick your objective, your targets, and upload your ad—done), other aspects of Facebook advertising confused me terribly. I did not understand how Facebook's algorithm worked because there wasn't much transparency about it at that time, and the rationale behind the 20 percent text rule eluded me because, if you ask other advertisers, the rule *wasn't applied consistently.* I also had a difficult time knowing the difference between a boosted post and a Facebook ad. Much like you are now, I was confused and frustrated.

But, I assure you, it will get better. In fact, you're off to a better start than I was because Facebook's platform has significantly improved in the last three years, and you have me to guide you through your first Facebook ad. If you still don't feel confident enough to create a Facebook ad, practice with a boosted post. It's the easiest ad to create, and it will allow you to become better acquainted with tools and options that you will have to use when creating ads on Ads Manager.

I have two pieces of advice I want to give to you before you start creating Facebook ads. First, expect to spend money. One of the things you have to do as a Facebook advertiser is to constantly test ads, and that requires spending. However, if done correctly (which you will be able to do after reading this book), Facebook advertising can be a valuable investment toward your business. Two, take it slow. Create one ad. Let it run. Then create another ad to outperform that ad. There are millions of elements you can test on Facebook, so it can quickly become overwhelming if you don't take it slow. In this chapter, I'll show you the steps you must take to create your first Facebook ad, from choosing an objective to choosing a format.

Choosing an Objective

When creating a Facebook ad, you must first choose an objective. This is such a vital part of your campaign that *Facebook won't allow you to skip it*. If you try skipping to the other levels of ad creation, you'll quickly find that you can't. Before you even dare begin creating a Facebook ad, know your campaign objective. Do you want to send people to your brick-and-mortar store? Do you want more brand exposure? Would you rather watch money flow into your account as you garner more sales? Facebook wants you to choose an objective before you create your ad because different objectives have different eligible ad placements and formats. For example, only an ad with the objective store visits can feature an ad with a map that directs customers to your location. In this section, I discuss all the objectives available to you—their purposes, their placements, and their eligible ad formats.

Figure 7.1 Objective options

Brand Awareness

Here's an interesting question for you: would you feel more comfortable doing a friend or a stranger a favor? You likely chose the former option, a completely reasonable choice. Of course, you'd rather choose your friend, someone you shared adventures, laughs, and drinks with. Who wouldn't? This goes the same for Facebook ads—users will be more likely to buy from you once they've familiarized with your brand. For this reason, it's often wise to begin with a brand awareness campaign, especially if your brand is not well known.

The brand awareness objective, which aims to increase the recall of ads rather than to generate sales, will help you find customers most likely to recall your ads and customers who will most likely purchase from you in the future. Although you likely won't generate sales, you will, instead, gain a higher ad recall lift. Don't think a brand awareness campaign is a waste of money because it *will* pay off in the end. Once you track conversions with your Facebook pixel, you can then retarget to those who converted—that is, those who, after getting acquainted with your brand, will be more likely to purchase from you.

Eligible placements: mobile and desktop news feeds, Instant Articles, in-stream videos, suggested videos, Instagram feed, Audience Network

Eligible formats: video, carousel, image, slideshow

Reach

If you want to show your ad to the maximum number of people in your audience, you should choose the reach objective. This objective differs from the previously mentioned brand awareness objective: optimizing for brand awareness means showing ads to only those who are likely to pay attention, whereas optimizing for reach means showing ads to everyone.

Eligible placements: mobile and desktop news feeds, in-stream videos, Instagram feed, Instagram Stories, Audience Network

Eligible formats: video, carousel, image, slideshow

Traffic

Maybe brand awareness and reach are not the objectives you're looking for. Maybe you'd rather send users to your website so they can learn more about your business, contact you, or purchase your products. If so, then traffic is the objective of your choice. With the traffic objective, you can direct customers to your website, encouraging them to explore your content and familiarize themselves with your business.

Eligible placements: mobile and desktop news feeds, Instant Articles, suggested videos, Instagram feed, Audience Network, right column

Eligible formats: video, carousel, image, slideshow format

Engagement

There's nothing more disheartening than watching your posts generate little to no engagement. You check your app almost every hour (even at work), hoping that someone, anyone, showed your post some love. If your post, page, or event is suffering from embarrassingly low engagement, the engagement objective is the answer to your prayers. With this objective, which encourages your audience to react to your post, page, or event, your engagement will go from scant to bountiful.

High engagement doesn't just inflate your ego, although it does give you a nice confidence boost. It also functions as social proof that gives your brand credibility. Let's say you're browsing for a law firm you want to hire. You see two candidates' Facebook pages. One has a thousand likes, whereas the other one only has a hundred. You choose the one with a thousand likes because, you think to yourself, only a business with approval from so many people is competent and, consequently, worth your money. Engagement may be, as some marketers call it, a vanity metric, but it's still valuable to your brand because it gives it credibility.

Eligible placements: mobile and desktop news feeds, Instant Articles, in-stream videos, right column, suggested videos, Instagram feed, Audience Network

Eligible formats: image

App Installs

Although numerous Facebook objectives exist, if you want users to install your app, the only—and the best—objective available to you is the app installs objective, with which you can create an ad that directs users to your ready-to-download app. You can't use a different objective for app installs because the app installs objective is the only one that allows you to include a link to your app. With the app installs objective, you can do the following:

· Increase the number of people who install your app by directing them to the Apple App store or the Google Play store.

· Increase engagement from existing customers by encouraging them to use your app again (which can include directing them to a specific place within your app).

Eligible placements: mobile and desktop news feeds, Instant Articles, suggested videos, Instagram feed, Audience Network

Eligible formats: video, carousel, image, slideshow

Video Views

I'm lucky enough that I have an amazing, talented VP of creative on my team who produces daily award-winning videos for my very pleased clients. He works tirelessly each day, editing and perfecting videos over and over *and over* again. If you also have a talented VP of creative whose videos you want to promote on Facebook or if you simply want to promote a video you're proud of, you're in luck—there's an objective for that. Granted, you can use the video ad format for several different objectives, such as brand awareness, traffic, and reach. However, choosing the video views objective for your video ad is different because the focus will be on garnering views rather than sales (if you choose traffic as your objective) or leads (if you choose lead generation).

Eligible placements: mobile and desktop news feeds, Instant Articles, in-stream videos, suggested videos, Instagram feed, Instagram Stories, Audience Network, right column

Eligible formats: video, carousel, slideshow

Lead Generation

If you want to run a lead generation campaign or to collect customer information on Facebook, then you should use the lead generation objective. With this objective, you can create an ad that, once clicked, opens into a prefilled form. In the form, you can ask almost any question you want as long as it complies with Facebook's ad policies and your privacy policy. You can ask users for their email address, full name, phone number, and location, just to name a few examples. (I'll go into more detail about lead ads in chapter 8.)

Eligible placements: mobile and desktop news feeds, Instagram feed

Eligible formats: single image, single video, carousel, slideshow

Conversions

If you want people to make a desired action on your website, then you should choose conversions as your objective. With this objective, you can urge customers to purchase, add credit card information, or browse through your products. Conversions work differently from traffic because, although the traffic objective optimizes for website traffic (getting people to visit your website), conversions optimize for conversions (desired actions).

Eligible placements: mobile and desktop news feeds, Instant Articles, Instagram feed, Instagram Stories, Audience Network, right column

Eligible formats: single video, single image, carousel, slideshow, collection

Product Catalog Sales

If you choose promote a product catalog as your objective, you will be able to create dynamic ads, ads that automatically advertise products from your product catalog. Dynamic ads work especially well if you target customers who have browsed through your catalog but have not yet purchased an item. The pixel will track which pages of your website a customer visited (i.e., product catalog or checkout) and, based on its findings, will serve a relevant ad to that customer. For example, if your customer looked at a fur coat from your catalog, your ad will automatically advertise that same product to your customer without your needing to create a new ad. Dynamic ads are great tools that push interested customers to make a purchase.

Eligible placements: mobile and desktop news feeds, right column, Instagram feed, Audience Network

Eligible formats: single image, carousel

Store Visits

If you own a chain store, you likely have multiple stores in various locations. If you want to simultaneously promote your multiple physical stores from different locations in one ad, then you should choose the store visits objective. An ad with a store visits objective will direct your customers to a physical store that is nearest to their current location. Based on the CTA you chose (get directions or call now), the ad will contain either a map that will navigate customers to your nearest store or contact information that customers can use to contact your business.

Eligible placements: mobile and desktop news feeds

Eligible formats: single image, single video, carousel, slideshow

Creating Your Target Audience

Facebook's ad targeting is the reason I quit my nine-to-five and started my agency. I saw its potential, and I jumped on it. I saw laser-precision targeting that I never saw before in all of my years as an advertiser, targeting that can be so unbelievably precise and detailed that it's almost omniscient. With more than 850 targeting options, you can target almost anyone, anywhere, and in almost any walk of life. You can target people of any gender, any interest, and in any location—in the United States, Canada, or the Philippines. Facebook's targeting almost has no limits. However, with great power comes great responsibility, so you should always refer to Facebook's ad policy when you create your target audience. (I talk more about Facebook's ad policy in chapter 15.)

Facebook, as I mentioned earlier in the book, created targeting options from self-reported data and third-party data. Self-reported data comes from the information Facebook users provide on Facebook. This includes all information they provide on their profiles, such as occupation, education, relationship status, and interests. Third-party data, conversely, comes from third-party data brokers, such as Acxiom, Epsilon, Experian, Oracle Data Cloud, TransUnion, and WPP, that provide consumer data, including household income, home value, and purchasing behaviors.

With Facebook's vast targeting options—and your eagerness to obtain a large audience—you will likely try to target as many people as you can, but don't do that. Bigger is not always better, and that adage rings true for ad targeting. When you target an audience, the median is key. You have to make sure that your audience is neither too broad nor too narrow. The former can result in targeting people who aren't interested in your business, whereas the latter can result in excluding high-interest, potential customers. To check whether your audience is too big or too small, refer to the audience-size meter that appears on the left side of your screen.

Figure 7.2 The audience-size meter

When creating a target audience, you have two options: you can create a new audience or you can upload a customer list (called a custom audience in Facebook's world, but more on that later). If you don't have a customer list, then you should create a new audience. You have several targeting options for creating a new audience: demographics, connections, interests, behaviors, custom audience, and lookalike audience.

Demographics

When you create the demographics for your target audience, you can choose from a large variety of options. You can choose the basic options, such as location, age, gender, and language; however, you shouldn't stop there. For a more effective target audience, you should also include detailed targeting, such as education level, job title, relationship status, political views, home type, and financial situation. Simply type the keyword related to the demographic you want to target into the search box for detailed targeting, and it will appear. If not, then that option is not available.

Figure 7.3 Demographics section

Connections

You can also target an audience according to its connection with your business. You can target people or friends of those people who either liked your Facebook pages, used your apps, or responded to your events. Conversely, you can exclude anyone who has any connections with your business. Unlike the detailed targeting for demographics and interests, which you access by entering keywords into the detailed targeting search box, connections targeting appears as a drop-down menu on the bottom of the audience section.

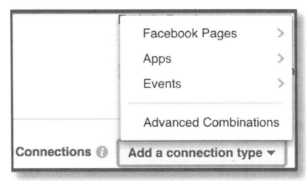

Figure 7.4 Connection types

Interests

There are hundreds of options for interest targeting, which includes hobbies and activities, entertainment, business and industry, sports, shopping, fashion, food and drink, fitness, and wellness. You can target certain interests by typing the keyword for the interest you want to target in the detailed targeting search box. You can differentiate between a suggestion that is under the interests category and a suggestion that is under the demographics category by looking at the category label next to the suggestions. If it's an interest targeting option, it should be labeled "interests."

Target audiences differ according to different targeting categories. For example, if you typed "energy drinks" and clicked an interest targeting option, Facebook will send the ad to people who have expressed interest in energy drinks on Facebook (e.g., following or liking an energy drink page). If, instead, you clicked a behavior targeting option, Facebook will send the ad to people who are known to be or likely to be buyers of energy drinks based on their purchase behavior. To make sure you're targeting the people you want, double check that the option you're choosing is from the correct category.

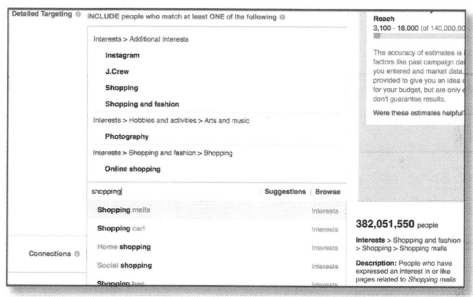

Figure 7.5 Interest targeting options

Behaviors

Behavior targeting exists because of the data third-party partners provide. These partners know what people are doing offline: what products they buy, how much money they make, and which retail stores they visit. Because of third-party data, which made behavior targeting possible, you can create a target audience based on people's purchase behaviors (what and where people buy), financial behaviors (which card type people use to buy), and traveling behaviors (which airlines people fly use when they travel and whether they fly for business or for leisure). You can choose from Facebook's numerous behavioral targeting options from the detailed targeting search box. When you type the keywords for your chosen behavior, several suggestions will appear. Make sure to click the keyword that is labeled "behavior."

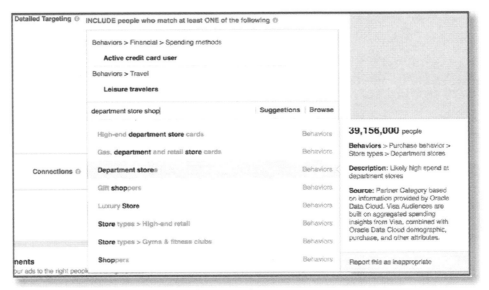

Figure 7.6 Behavioral targeting options

Custom Audiences

A custom audience, which eliminates the inconvenience of looking for new customers by targeting existing ones, is an ad targeting tool that allows you to direct ads to your existing contact list, which may be a list of customers taken from lead ads and sign-ups. Facebook will compare the list you uploaded with its data to find the people in your list on its platform. You can add a custom audience to your targeting by clicking the custom audience text box. A list of your existing custom audiences should appear.

Figure 7.7 The area from which to upload Custom Audiences

Creating a custom audience is important for two reasons. First, it can garner more conversions by targeting users who are already in your customer list, have proven to be loyal customers, and are already interested in your business. In contrast, if you no longer want to advertise to the people in your list (such a situation would occur if you were to create a brand awareness campaign, targeting only those who have never interacted with your business), you can exclude your custom audience from your target audience. Second, you can use your custom audience to build a lookalike audience, which would allow you to target new users who are similar to your current customers.

Figure 7.8 Where to find audiences

Figure 7.9 The audiences page

Uploading a Custom Audience to Facebook

To create a custom audience, you must upload an Excel sheet filled with your customers' information. If this sheet is not formatted correctly, an error message will appear and prevent you from uploading your custom audience. To prevent complications, follow the Facebook formatting guidelines provided below.

Table 1. Facebook's Formatting Guideline

Data type	Column header	Description and formatting guidelines	Examples
Email	email	Facebook accepts up to three separate email address columns in US and international formats.	username@hotmail.co.uk your.name@gmail.com myname@yahoo.com
Phone Number	phone	Phone numbers must include a country code to be used for matching. For example, a 1 must precede a phone number in the United States. Facebook accepts up to three phone numbers as separate columns, with or without punctuation. Important: Always include the country code as part of your customer's phone numbers, even if all of your data is from the same country.	1-234-567-8910 12345678910 +44 844 412 4653
First Name	fn	Facebook accepts first name and first name initial, with or without accents. Initials can be provided with or without a period.	John F. Émilie
Last Name	ln	Facebook accepts full last names with or without accents.	Smith Sørensen Jacobs-Anderson
City	ct	Facebook accepts full city names as they normally appear.	Paris London New York
State/ Province	st	Facebook accepts full names of US and international states and provinces as well as the abbreviated versions of US states.	AZ California Normandy

Data type	Column header	Description and formatting guidelines	Examples
Country	country	Facebook accepts country names that are presented as an ISO two-letter country code. Important: Always include your customers' countries in their own column in your file, even if all of your data is from the same country. Because Facebook matches on a global scale, this simple step helps them match as many people as possible from their customer list.	FR US GB
Date of Birth	dob	Facebook accepts eighteen different date formats to accommodate a range of month, day, and year combinations, with or without punctuation.	MM-DD-YYYY MM/DD/YYYY MMDDYYYY DD-MM-YYYY DD/MM/YYYY DDMMYYYY YYYY-MM-DD YYYY/MM/DD YYYYMMDD MM-DD-YY MM/DD/YY MMDDYY DD-MM-YY DD/MM/YY DDMMYY YY-MM-DD YY/MM/DD
Year of Birth	doby	Facebook accepts year of birth as a four-digit number, YYYY.	1986

Data type	Column header	Description and formatting guidelines	Examples
Age	age	Facebook accepts age as a numerical value.	65 42 21
Zip/Postal Code	zip	Facebook accepts US and international zip and postal codes. US zip codes may include four-digit extensions as long as they are separated by a hyphen. The extension is not required and will not further improve match rate.	W11 2BQ 94104-1207 94104
Gender	gen	Facebook accepts an initial to indicate gender.	M F
Mobile Advertiser ID	madid	Facebook accepts two types of mobile advertiser IDs: Android's Advertising ID (AAID), which Google provides as part of Android advertising, and Apple's Advertising Identifier (IDFA), which Apple provides as part of iOS in its ads framework.	AECE52E7-03EE-455A-B3C4-E57283966239 BEBE52E7-03EE-455A-B3C4-E57283966239
Facebook App_User ID	uid	An ID corresponding to someone who uses an app that can be retrieved through the Facebook SDK. Facebook accepts numerical user IDs associated with your Facebook application.	

Uploading a Custom Audience

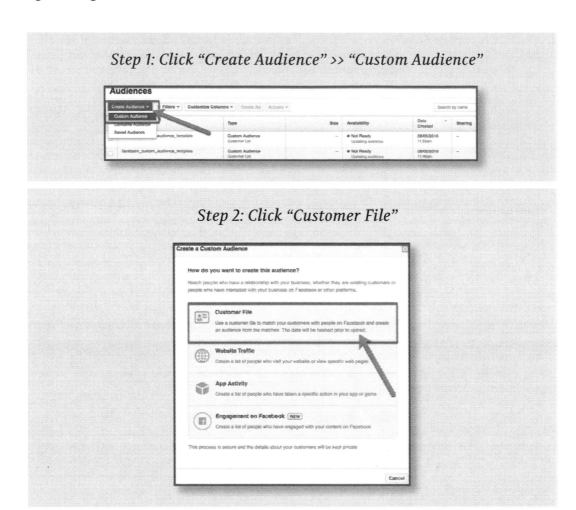

Step 1: Click "Create Audience" >> "Custom Audience"

Step 2: Click "Customer File"

Step 3: Click "Choose a file or copy and paste data"

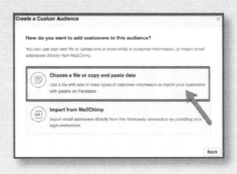

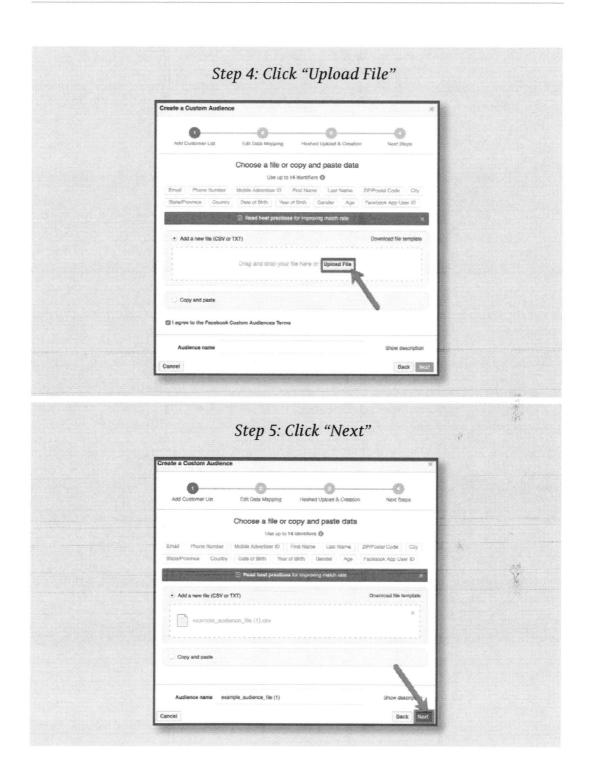

Step 6: Click "Upload & Create"

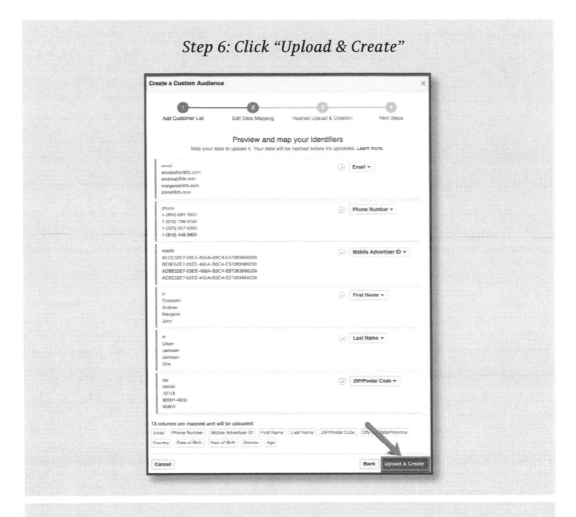

Step 7: Wait

Depending on your data size, upload time may be quick or slow.

Step 8: Click "Done" to finish

Other Types of Custom Audiences

The custom audience I showed you how to upload is a type of custom audience called customer file. There are three other custom audiences that you can use: website traffic, app activity, and engagement. Although the customer file custom audience requires a spreadsheet to create, these three other custom audiences only need one thing: a Facebook pixel. Once again, the Facebook pixel comes in handy as I repeatedly said it would be. The pixel's role in creating custom audiences is to gather information on customers and save it for your use. You then upload that information to custom audiences to create a new set of audience. Without a working pixel, you will be unable to create the website traffic, app activity, and engagement custom audiences.

- **Website traffic:** A custom audience of people who visited your website or took actions on your site (e.g., purchased, added to cart, or abandoned cart).

- **App activity:** A custom audience of people who used your app, among other specific actions.

- **Engagement on Facebook:** A custom audience of people who have engaged with your content on Facebook (e.g., your posts, ads, or events).

Lookalike Audience

Lookalike audience allows you to reach an audience that is similar to the people in your custom audience or to your Facebook page followers. From your uploaded custom audience or Facebook page, Facebook will identify common qualities between your audience and Facebook's users. Afterward, Facebook will serve your ad to people who are similar to the people in your custom audience and Facebook page followers in the location you choose. You can create lookalike audiences in the audiences section of Business Manager, the same page from which you created your custom audience.

Creating a Lookalike Audience

Step 1: Go to asset library >> audiences >> click "Create Audience" >>
"Lookalike Audience"

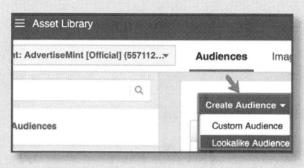

Step 2: Upload custom audience or Facebook page >> add location >>
add size >> click "Create Audience"

Creating a Value-Based Lookalike Audience

A value-based lookalike audience helps you serve ads to people who are similar to your highest value customers. To create a value-based lookalike audience, you must upload a custom audience that contains a customer lifetime value, or customer LTV, defined by Facebook as "a numeric representation of the net profit you predict [that] will be attributable to a given customer over the duration of your relationship with [that customer]." Here's how you create a value-based lookalike audience.

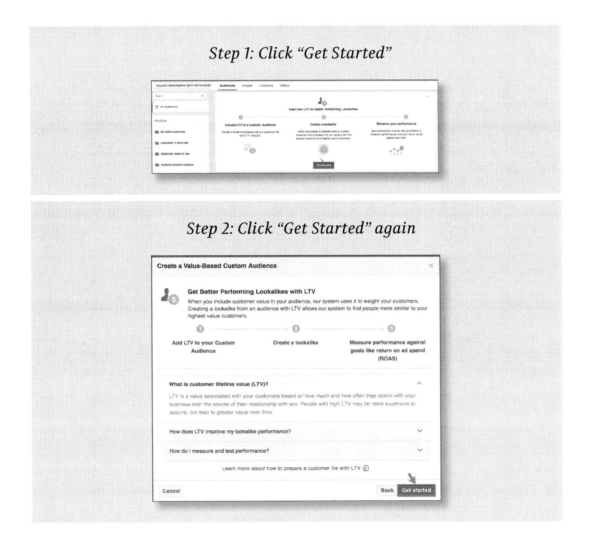

Step 3: Accept the terms

Step 4: Upload custom audience file >> "Next"

Step 5: Choose your customer value >> "Next"

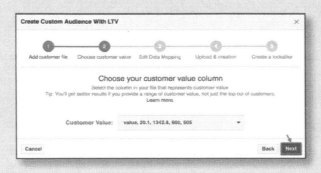

Step 6: Click "Upload & Create"

Step 7: Click "Create Lookalike"

Step 8: Create a Lookalike Audience

To create your lookalike audience, you must choose the location you want Facebook to find customers from. Next, you must choose an audience size, or the amount of people you want Facebook to find. Afterward, click "**Create Audience.**"

Step 9: You're done

Lookalike (US, 1%) - example_value_based_audience_file	Lookalike Value-based Custom Audience: ex...
example_value_based_audience_file	Custom Audience Customer List: Value-based

Choosing Your Ad Placements

After you choose your objective and target audience, the next step is to choose your placements, which are places where you can place your ads. For example, if you choose Instagram Stories as your placement, your ad will appear between users' stories. If you choose mobile news feed, your ad will appear on the Facebook app's news feed. You have two placement options to choose from: automatic and edit.

- **Automatic placements:** Facebook automatically selects the recommended placements your ads are eligible for, depending on your objective and creative. This is the default option.

Figure 7.10 Automatic Placements

- **Edit placements:** You manually choose your placements.

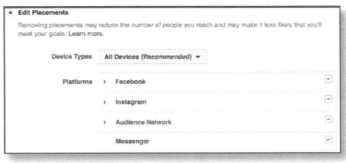

Figure 7.11 Edit Placements

Although Facebook offers six placements, some of your ads may not be eligible for all of them because eligibility depends on your advertising objective, as previously mentioned. For example, if you chose the objective mobile app installs, your ad will only be eligible for placement on Instagram, mobile news feed, and Audience Network. If your ad is ineligible for certain placements, it will say "ineligible" next to your placement. In this section, I discuss all of the placements available to you.

Figure 7.12 Examples of ineligible placements

Desktop News Feed

If you choose to place your ads on Facebook's desktop news feed, your ad will appear on news feed, the section of Facebook where posts by your friends and family appear. It's important to remember, however, that placing your ads on *desktop* news feed means your ads will only appear on news feeds accessed through desktop computers and laptops. Do not confuse this with mobile news feed, which is accessed through mobile phones.

Many advertisers favor desktop news feed ads because their resemblance to regular posts are more appealing to Facebook users, who hate intrusive ads, including pop-up ads and video ads that play automatically with sound on. Desktop news feed ads, on the contrary, blend with their environment and do not interrupt the user experience. Additionally, advertisers prefer news feed ads because they appear on the section of Facebook that receives the most attention; because posts appear on news feed, users' eyes are often glued to the feed, giving your ad a higher chance of being noticed. However, what works for some may not work for others. The best way to determine whether this placement is the best for you is to test it. If you find that other placements cost less and deliver the desired results, then desktop news feed is not the right placement for your ad. If you find contrary results, then you should stick with it.

Objectives eligible for this placement: Brand awareness, reach, traffic, engagement, app installs, video views, lead generation, conversions, product catalog sales, store visits

Mobile News Feed

When you choose to place your ad on Facebook's mobile news feed, your ad will appear on the app's news feed. Much like desktop news feed, your ad will appear among your friends and family's Facebook posts.

Some advertisers prefer placing their ads on mobile news feed for two reasons. First, there is a higher likelihood that people will see the ad. Because mobile news feed fills up an entire phone screen and because posts appear on the screen one at a time, people have no choice but to look at your ad when it appears. Unlike the desktop news feed, there is no left sidebar or right column to distract the eyes. Second, more people access Facebook through mobile. As of March 2017, Facebook has 1.94 billion monthly active users. Of those 1.94 billion users, 1.74 billion access Facebook only through mobile.[9] Thus, neglecting to place ads on mobile news feed means losing a large group of potential customers.

---

9   Facebook. Facebook Q3 2016 Results. 2016. Raw data. Investor.fb.com. Facebook's Q3 2016 Earnings Report.

Objectives eligible for this placement: brand awareness, reach, traffic, engagement, app installs, video views, lead generation, conversions, product catalog sales, store visits

Right Column

The Facebook right columns, also known as the right or left bars, appear on either sides of your news feed. The columns contain both important information and easily accessible actions. For instance, the left column contains actions such as creating a Facebook event, an ad, or a fundraiser; the right column contains trending topics and Facebook ads. If you want your ads to appear in the right column, then you should choose right column as your placement.

Figure 7.13 The right column on the right side of news feed

News feed ads trump sidebar ads in popularity, and for good reasons. Although right column ads were the only ads that Facebook allowed when it first debuted advertising on its platform, right column ads didn't generate the best results because they were located on the right column, which was rarely noticed. (In the first four years of using Facebook, I don't think I've ever clicked a right column ad once.) However, there are a few benefits to using the right column placement.

- Right column ads will rarely get negative feedback because they are not in the news feed.

- Right column ads are usually much cheaper than news feed ads because they are not placed in a highly coveted location.

- Right column ads usually work best with an older audience because an older audience will often be more inclined to browse the entire page. A younger audience, in contrast, is extremely quick and impatient, often skimming through content at the speed of light. If your ad is not right in front of a young audience's eyes, it will most likely be missed.

- Right column ads are less intrusive than news feed ads because they are separated from news feed where people's posts appear.

Figure 7.14 An example of a right column ad

When checking Facebook's news feeds as your placement, the right column will automatically be included *whether you want it or not*. Facebook claims that it needs all the placement options enabled in order to reach highly interested users at the lowest cost. Although this sounds like a reasonable explanation, remember that Facebook also profits from running your ads in all of the placements regardless of whether that placement is the best for generating your desired results.

You might be wondering which ad would be better—the news feed ad or the sidebar ad. Again, I cannot come to a conclusion for you because although some placements work for some advertisers, they may not work for others. For most of my clients, I often only use the right column with remarketing campaigns because remarketing ads target already interested users who are more likely to convert. However, because my focus is often on ROI for my clients, I normally favor news feed because it attracts the most attention, and it is a placement that users are more likely to notice and click on your ad. My advice is to test which placement works better for you.

Objectives eligible for this placement: engagement, product catalog sales, traffic, video views, conversions

Audience Network

The Audience Network, a partnership between Facebook and publishers, allows you to reach more people by placing ads on the apps and websites of Facebook's partners. For instance, Target, which wanted to target those who use their app and those who want to watch *Frozen*, found their audience through the *Huffington Post's* mobile app. In another example, Audible, which wanted to promote its *Game of Thrones* audiobooks to fans, found its audience through the Cut the Rope app.

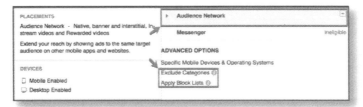

Figure 7.15 Where to exclude categories and upload block lists

Audience Network's ability to connect you with an audience that you may not find on Facebook, giving your brand omnipresence in your customers' online experience, has been proven to work. I've read several success stories, and two of them, I remember, were successes from the US Navy and Rosetta Stone. When the US Navy chose to serve ads to Audience Network, its campaign reach soared to 33 percent. When Rosetta Stone followed the same strategy in an attempt to drive installs of its mobile app, it reduced cost per impression by almost 40 percent. Their success is not surprising considering Facebook has the ability to connect businesses with one billion people and has several new partners, including Univision, *Washington Post*, Wenner Media, *Daily Mirror*, and BBM, among many others.

Unfortunately, you do not have the power to choose which publishers and devices you can place your ads in. However, you can exclude certain categories, or the type of content, you don't want your ads to appear alongside of, as shown in figure 6.13. The categories are dating, debatable social issues, gambling, mature, and tragedy and conflict. If there's a specific website or app you don't want your ad to appear alongside of, you can also create block lists by uploading a .txt or .csv list of website domains and app store URLs that you want to block.

Creating Block Lists

Step 1: Go to "Business Settings" >> "People and Assets" >> "Block Lists"

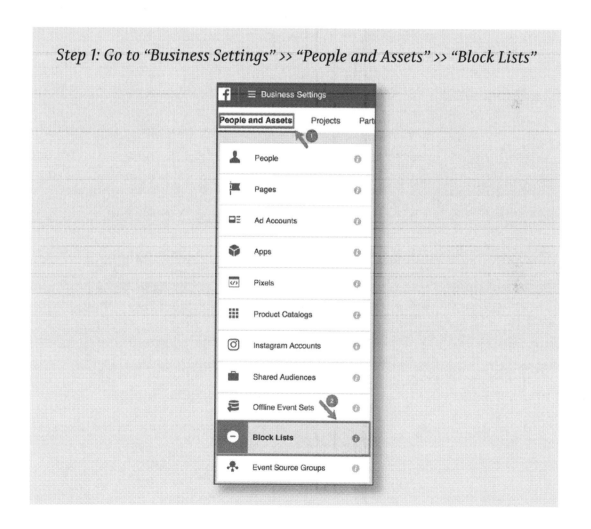

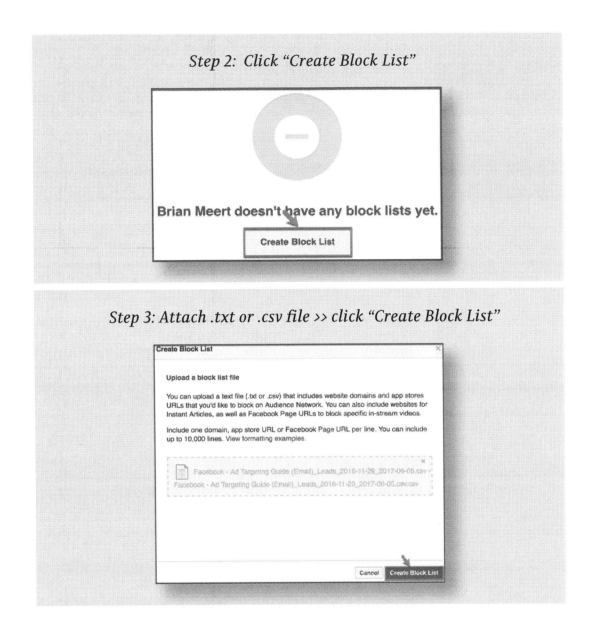

You can upload your block list to your ad at the ad set level by clicking "**Apply Block Lists**" under advanced options, as also shown in figure 6.13.

Objectives eligible for this placement: brand awareness, reach, traffic, engagement, app installs, video views, conversions, product catalog sales

Instant Articles

Have you ever had to wait too long for an article that you accessed through a social networking app to load? Facebook solved that problem in 2015 when it launched Instant Articles, a feature that makes articles load easily in its mobile app. When Facebook users click on an article, the article opens within Facebook's app with similar formatting to the article on the publisher's website.

If you choose Instant Articles as your placement, you're placing ads between the paragraphs of the articles that people read on Facebook's app. Much like Audience Network, Instant Articles gives your brand omnipotence as it follows your users from news feed to the articles they're reading. Unfortunately, you can't choose which publishers' websites to place your ads on. But you can, however, block categories and create block lists as you would with Audience Network.

Figure 7.16 Where to find the Instant Articles placement

Objectives eligible for this placement: video views, traffic, conversions, engagement, app installs, product catalog sales

Instagram Feed

When you place your ad on Instagram's feed, your ad will appear among Instagram users' posts. You can place eligible Facebook ads on Instagram without having to create or adjust your creative. Note that Instagram does not support all of Facebook's ad formats. Although single image, video, and carousel ads are eligible for placement on Instagram, canvas and slideshow ads are not.

If you want to tell your brand's story at the center of a visual representation, then I recommend placement on Instagram, a platform that focuses on visually focused content. To ensure that your ad successfully blends in with Instagram's environment, you must use professional, creative, high-quality, and visually appealing photos and videos for your ads. Take a few minutes to browse through brands' Instagram feeds to get acquainted with the type of content they usually post on Instagram.

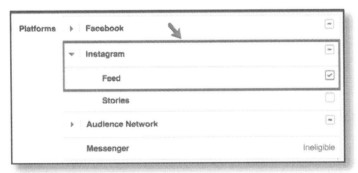

Figure 7.17 The Instagram feed and Stories placement

Objectives eligible for this placement: brand awareness, reach, traffic, engagement, app installs, video views, lead generation, conversions, product catalog sales

Instagram Stories

When you place ads on Instagram Stories, your vertical ads will appear between Instagram users' ephemeral ten-second stories. Usually, when you create an ad, you can place ads on multiple placements. For example, I can place ads on Instagram's feed, Facebook's feed, and Audience Network simultaneously. That is not the case for placement on Stories. You can't use other placements alongside Instagram Stories because Stories ads require ad specs that are incompatible with other ad formats and placements. For instance, all Stories ads must be in a vertical video format, a format that is not compatible for all the other placements. If you want to place ads on Instagram Stories, plan to create separate creatives exclusively for Stories.

Figure 7.18
An Instagram
Stories ad

If you want to show your ads to the maximum number of Instagram users in your audience and generate a larger brand awareness, then choose the Instagram Stories placement.

Objectives eligible for this placement: reach, video views, conversions, product catalog sales

In-Stream Video

You can place five- to fifteen-second video ads within live and non-live videos on Facebook by choosing the in-stream video placement.

When in-stream placement first launched, many advertisers felt apprehensive about using it because they were afraid their ads would appear within inappropriate content that they did not want associated with their brand. Content that was a cause for worry included adult, dating, and political content. If you don't want your ad to appear alongside certain types of content, you can include your block list in your ad or block certain categories as you would with placements on Audience Network.

Objectives eligible for this placement: brand awareness, engagement, video views

Choosing Your Budget and Schedule

The next step is to create your budget and schedule, which you can do at the ad set level. So many curious advertisers and potential clients ask me how much Facebook ads cost. Here's the thing: Facebook doesn't have a fixed fee for its ads because the ad buying process is a bid. Rather than charging you a set amount per month, Facebook charges you by the amount you're willing to pay. Do you want to spend $20 a day? You can do that. Do you want to spend $5 a day? You can do that too. You establish your budget with Facebook, and Facebook will charge you within your budget. There's no maximum daily spend you need to abide by, but I don't recommend that you cheap out on your ads. You have to bid for a spot for Facebook's platform, after all, and throwing in a few dollars helps you win a good spot. In this section you'll learn how to create your budget and schedule.

Budget

Your budget is the amount of money you're willing to pay over the period of time you chose your ads to run. In the example below, I have a $20 daily budget, which means I'll spend a maximum of $20 each day. Although I have $20 to spend each day, I may not necessarily have to spend that entire budget. For example, Facebook may decide to charge me $15 on one day or $5 on another. Although the charge per day may differ, Facebook will never charge you more than your daily budget.

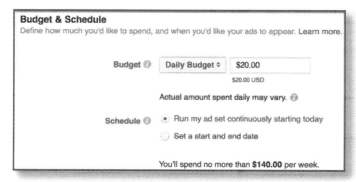

Figure 7.19 Setting your budget and schedule

When setting a budget, you have the option to choose between a daily budget and a lifetime budget. Your daily budget is the amount you're willing to spend each day, and your lifetime budget is the amount you're willing to spend over the duration of your ad set. Once you've chosen a budget type, you can't switch to a different one while the ad is running. You can, however, duplicate an ad set and create a different budget type for that ad set.

Schedule

After you've set your budget, you must then choose your schedule. Your default option is to run your ad set continuously. If you select that option, Facebook will run your ads until your budget has been completely spent. Your second option is to set a start and end date. Facebook will run your ad based on the start date that you choose and end it on the end date that you choose. The times entered must comply with the times of each ad's location. Thus, if you start your ads targeted in New York and London at 5:00 p.m., both ads will begin at 5:00 p.m. in their respective locations.

Figure 7.20 Choosing your schedule

Optimization for Ad Delivery

When you optimize for ad delivery, you're telling Facebook which delivery you value the most. You have three options: click, impressions, and reach.

· **Click:** Facebook will deliver your ad to an audience that is most likely to click on your link at the lowest cost.

· **Impressions:** Facebook will place your ad in front of your audience as frequently as possible.

· **Reach:** Facebook will deliver your ad to your audience once a day.

Different ad objectives work well with different optimizations. For example, an ad with the traffic objective would work well with an optimization for clicks, whereas an ad with the brand awareness objective would work well with an optimization for impressions. When choosing your optimization, keep your objective in mind.

Figure 7.21 Options for ad delivery optimization

Bid Amount

Facebook advertising is an auction in which advertisers bid against each other to obtain a spot on Facebook's platform. Your bid amount represents your level of interest in showing your ads: low bids show low interest; high bids show high interest. There are two ways you can set your bid. First, you can set it on automatic and allow Facebook to bid on your behalf. Second, you can set it on manual and choose the amount of money you're willing to pay per 1,000 impressions. My advice: choose automatic bid if you don't have a set value in mind and choose manual bid if you know how much you're willing to pay per bid. If you do choose manual bid, *don't bid too low*. Remember that Facebook advertising is an auction. If you bid too low, your competitors *will* outbid you for the spot that you want.

Figure 7.22 Setting the bid amount

When You Get Charged

You have two options for when you want Facebook to charge you. You can choose to be charged every time 1,000 impressions occur or every time someone clicks on your ad. If you choose per 1,000 impressions, Facebook will charge you every time your ad appears on your audience's screen. If you choose link clicks, Facebook will charge you every time someone clicks on any part of your ad. This includes clicking to react, to comment, to share, or to claim your offer. If you're unsure which method would be more financially beneficial to you, you can test two different ad sets: one in which you're charged per impressions and one in which you're charged per clicks. See which ad is more inexpensive and continue to run that one.

Figure 7.23 Options for how Facebook charges you

Ad Scheduling

If you chose a lifetime budget, you'll have the option to either run your ads continuously or to run them according to a schedule. Running your ads on a schedule would be helpful if you knew when your audience is most often on Facebook, information that you can access through audience insights. Let's say audience insights shows me that my audience accesses Facebook from noon to 1:00 p.m. on the weekdays. To ensure that my audience sees my ads, I then schedule my ads to run every weekday from noon to 1:00 p.m.

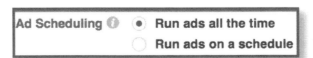

Figure 7.24 Ad scheduling options

Delivery Type

After you've paid for your ad and after Facebook has approved it, Facebook will deliver your ad to your target audience using two methods: standard delivery and accelerated delivery. If you choose standard delivery, the recommended delivery type, Facebook will deliver your ads evenly over the course of your campaign (this process is also called pacing). When choosing this option, keep in mind that, because Facebook paces your budget, Facebook may lower your bid when there are more inexpensive opportunities available to get the best results out of your budget. Pacing is advantageous to you because you will have the funds to spend on more inexpensive opportunities that may come later.

Figure 7.25 Delivery options

If you choose accelerated delivery, Facebook will deliver your ads as quickly as possible. The focus will be on speed rather than efficiency. Although this option may prevent you from getting the most statistical value from your ads (aka the most cost-effective delivery options), it will be beneficial to you if your campaign is time sensitive.

Sometimes you might find, to your utter shock and horror, that your ad is not delivering. That's because your ad doesn't have the highest total value, a value that is calculated by four factors: your bid, your ad quality and relevance, and your estimated action rates. The following is a checklist of what you can do to increase your highest total value:

1. **Enter a decent bid:** Although you can bid any amount you want, it's important not to bid too low. If a competitor bid a higher amount for a spot in a news feed that you want, you will lose the bid and the spot.

2. **Create high-quality ads:** Low-quality ads may affect delivery.

3. **Target a relevant audience:** If you target the wrong audience, an audience that isn't relevant to your offer (for example, targeting young women for an ad that advertises men's briefs), you will receive a low relevance score, which will result in low estimated action rates, the number of people Facebook predicts will respond to your ad.

It's important that your ad has a high total value; otherwise, your ad will not deliver.

Estimated Daily Results

As you're creating your ad in the ad set level, you will likely notice a square on the right column of your screen labeled "Estimated Daily Results." That square gives you an estimate of your daily reach and results based on your ad settings, such as your target audience, budget, and optimization. You'll notice that after you've chosen your objective, placement, schedule, and budget and created your audience, the estimated daily results bar will give you a predicted outcome based on what your campaign is optimized for.

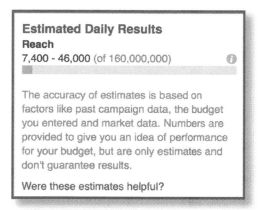

Figure 7.26 Facebook's estimated daily results

With the estimated daily results prediction, you can adjust your daily budget, optimize ad set performance, and use the information of your ad set that you have so far to improve your results. Estimated daily results are best suited for advertisers who have actions (e.g., video views, conversions, and installs) as their objective.

Choosing a Page

Figure 7.27 Connecting your page to your ad

As you move from the ad set level to the ad level, you will find a small section that requires you to connect a Facebook page or an Instagram account to your ad. Although small, you must not skip this section because the page you choose will represent the ad that appears on Facebook's platform and Audience Network. For example, by choosing my company's business page, the ad I created will appear as an ad from AdvertiseMint. If you're also placing your ads on Instagram, you're required to connect your Instagram account so that the ad will appear on Instagram's feed as represented by your business (the Instagram account you choose to connect).

Choosing Your Format

When I first started advertising, I used nothing but single image ads. However, I soon realized that in order to keep my audience interested in my ads, I needed to use other types of ad formats. My team's Facebook representative kept badgering us to create more video ads in almost every meeting. Finally, I relented and started producing video ads for my bigger clients—and he was right. Our results were great. When it comes to Facebook advertising, it's best to use more than one format to avoid ad fatigue, a phenomenon in which an audience that has seen your ads too many times overlooks or ignores your ads. Here, I'll show you the available ad formats, which you can access at the ad level.

Figure 7.28 Available ad formats

Single Image

Facebook's single image ad is an ad format that contains a text, a single image, a headline, a link description, and a CTA button.

Figure 7.29 The anatomy of a single image ad

The Text

The text appears above the image, usually containing details about your product or service, a value proposition, and a CTA. The text should convey everything your audience needs to know about the ad. What does it offer? What should your audience expect upon clicking the ad?

The recommended character count for the text is ninety characters. Note, however, that this is only a recommendation, not a requirement. Although fewer characters are often recommended by advertisers and copywriters alike, you are more than welcome to write longer texts. As always, A/B test which text length garners the best results.

The Image

Below the text is the ad's image. You can choose any image you want for your ad as long as it complies with Facebook's advertising policies, one of which requires that the text doesn't occupy more than 20 percent of the image, and ad specs. You can choose a product image, an image with a model, or an image with your brand's logo, among many other choices. Although you are free to choose any image, remember that your image must relate to your message. For example, if you're promoting your wine collection, use an image containing a few bottles of wine or an image with a model drinking, holding, or pouring wine into a glass.

The Headline

The headline, which appears below the image in bold, contains more information about the offer. It should be able to catch your audience's attention and compel them to click on your ad. In Gap's ad, the headline "Beat the holiday rush" encourages customers to shop early online for the holidays. Facebook recommends that you keep your character count to twenty-five characters for your headline.

The Link Description

The link description contains the description of the link you're providing on your ad. In figure 7.30, the link description "free same-day shipping" lets customers know that the ad's link will direct them to a product catalog where they can purchase products with free same-day shipping.

The CTA Button

The CTA button, located on the bottom-right corner of the ad, encourages people to take a desired action. In Gap's ad, the CTA button encourages customers to shop at its online store. Note that your CTA button must relate to your message. Don't, for example, use a "learn more" CTA when your ad's purpose is to drive customers to make a purchase. Using an irrelevant CTA will confuse, irritate, and disappoint customers when you don't meet their expectations at the landing page.

Single Video

Facebook's video ad, much like its image ad, is an ad format that contains a text, a headline, a link description, a CTA button, and, unlike the image ad, a video. All of the ad elements are located in the same area as the ad elements on an image ad. The text is above the video, which is then followed by the headline, the description, and the CTA button.

Figure 7.30 The anatomy of a single video ad

The Video

You can choose any video you want as long as it complies with Facebook's policies. Although you are free to upload any video to your ad, remember that your video must relate to your message. For example, if you're promoting a horror movie, use the movie's trailer for your video ad.

When choosing your video, make sure it complies with Facebook's ad specs and technical requirements. Although all uploaded videos have a maximum length of 120 minutes, try to keep your videos no longer than one minute to maintain your audience's attention, unless you're promoting a trailer, which are usually two to three minutes long. If you must use a video that's longer than one minute, make sure the heart of your message appears before the one-minute mark. Otherwise, you could lose your audience's interest. And, as always, A/B test to see which video length garners the best results.

When you create your video ad, make sure to design for sound off because most users prefer to watch their videos without sound. Although Facebook is currently rolling out a sound on option in which videos automatically play with sound, users can still opt out of this feature, and honestly, they most likely will. (The sound on feature is not popular among users.) Also, make sure you use high-quality videos. When creating your video, use these recommended custom settings:

- H.264 video with AAC audio in MOV or MP4 format

- An aspect ratio no larger than 1280px wide and divisible by 16px

- A frame rate at, or below, 30fps

- Stereo audio with a sample rate of 44,100hz

Carousel

Growing tired of creating those all-too-common single image ads day after day? Do you long to craft something new, something exciting, something that is practical yet aesthetically pleasing, complex yet easy to create? Behold Facebook's carousel ad. A carousel ad, unlike your regular single image ad, can feature up to ten images or videos that Facebook users can scroll through. Each card contains a clickable link to your

Figure 7.31
An example of a
carousel ad

landing page, a headline, and, if desired, a call-to-action button. If you choose to create a carousel ad, you will be able to display multiple products, tell a story, and showcase one long image through successive carousel ad cards in one ad unit.

You have a few placement and objective choices with carousel ads. You can choose to place these ads on Facebook's mobile and desktop news feed and Instagram. Because of its size, appearance, and function, the carousel ad cannot be placed on Facebook's right column. Carousel ads are eligible for ads with the objectives website clicks, website conversions, app installs, app engagement, video views, and page post engagement.

Canvas

Canvas ads don't just sell—they take you to an immersive, interactive experience. Unlike Facebook's single image ad or carousel ad, canvas ads, once clicked, unfold to full-screen view on your mobile phone. Once you're in the world of canvas, you can swipe up, down, left, right, or zoom in and out to follow the ad's narrative. Each of the ad's creative, whether it be an image or a video, can, if desired, include links to your landing

Figure 7.32
An example of a canvas ad

page, call-to-action buttons, and headlines. With a canvas ad, you can link multiple canvases for a microsite-like effect, choose a combination of capabilities to better tell your story, sequence your story to drive customers through your marketing funnel, and remarket to high-interest customers who opened your canvas. If you want to create a canvas ad, make sure to use one of the following objectives:

- Website clicks

- Website conversions

- Mobile app installs

- Mobile app engagement

- Video views

- Brand awareness

- Page post engagement

It's possible that you haven't seen a canvas ad on your news feed before—it's not hard to imagine why. Unlike your regular single image, video, slideshow, and carousel ads, canvas ads are more complex and more expensive to create. Businesses' apprehension of creating canvas ads likely explains its absence on Facebook. However, that does not indicate that canvas ads are ineffective ads. In fact, many bigger companies such as Coca Cola, Lowe's, and ASUS have used canvas ads with success. If you want an ad that's immersive, visual, and fast, then canvas ads are the ads for you.

Slideshow

In 2015, two events were occurring in the digital advertising scene: video was gaining popularity among Facebook users and users were consuming most of their video content on mobile. The popularity of video and users' shift from desktop to mobile presented several problems for advertisers: advertisers with a smaller budget could not afford to create and serve video ads, and those who could afford it

Figure 7.33
An example of a slideshow ad

had difficulty delivering their ads to a cell phone-using audience living in areas with low Wi-Fi speeds and to an audience that owned older cell phone models. To combat these predicaments, Facebook created slideshow ads, lightweight ads that are easier and more inexpensive for businesses to create, ads that load and play easily in areas with low internet speeds and for those with older cell phone models.

Slideshow is a lightweight video ad created from a series of three to ten still images. You can use images from video stills, a photo shoot, or photos from Facebook's free photo library. Slideshow can also include music, as long as the music you upload is licensed for use. Slideshows can be as short as five seconds and as long as fifty seconds.

Adding Your Media, Text, Links, and Pixel

The last step in the ad level is to add your media, text, links, and pixel. The media section is where you can add the media for your ad, whether that's an image for your image ads or a video for your videos ads (figure 6.28). Next, you need to write the copies for your ad. You must write copies for your text, headline, and link description (figure 6.29). When writing your copies, make sure they are grammatically correct, relevant to your overall offer, and concise.

Figure 7.34 Where to add your media

Once you've added your media and copies, you must include your website URL (figure 6.29). This is the destination your ad will send your customers to. For example, if I wanted my customers to know about AdvertiseMint's services, I would add the URL that directly sends my customers to AdvertiseMint's services page. Always check that your website link matches your ad's description. For example, *don't* advertise your product catalog and, instead of providing the URL to your product catalog, add the URL for your about page. Doing so will direct your customers to a page that they did not expect, causing them to feel deceived.

Next, you must choose your CTA button, display link, and pixel options (figure 6.29). When choosing your CTA button, you must make sure that it describes the action you want your customers to take and that it is relevant to your landing page. For example, if the website URL you provided will direct them to your product catalog, and you want your customer to make a purchase from that product catalog, then you should choose "Shop Now" or "Buy Now" as your CTA button. The display link, conversely, is the link that appears on the ad. Although this feature may not appear on all placements,

Figure 7.35
Where to add links,
text, and CTA

placements such as Facebook news feed will show the display link to customers. Finally, you must choose to track conversions from your Facebook pixel (figure 6.30). Although it's optional to track conversions with your pixel, I highly recommend that you do so. I cannot stress enough the importance of pixel tracking. Before you submit your ad for Facebook's approval, always check that you enabled pixel tracking.

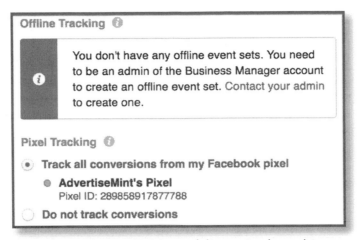

Figure 7.36 enabling pixel tracking

As you're editing from the ad level, you will see a preview of your ad on the right side of your screen. You can click the dropdown menu above it to preview your ad in other placements. Once you're satisfied with your ad, you can click "Place Order" to submit your ad to Facebook. Once approved, you will receive an email notification.

CHAPTER 8: CREATING SPECIAL ADS

In the previous chapter, I taught you how to create a Facebook ad. I taught you how to choose an objective, create a target audience, set your budget and schedule, and choose your format. These are the steps you *will always have to take* when creating any type of ad, whether that's a lead ad, a single image ad, or a slideshow ad. However, some ads require you to take extra steps. For example, when creating a lead ad, you have to create a lead form. Or, if you want to create a store-visits ad, you would have to set a store location. In this chapter, I will guide you through creating special ads, or ads that require a unique extra step.

Lead Ads

If you want more leads, you're in luck—there's an ad for that. Behold the lead ad, an ad that lets you collect valuable information from potential customers without directing them outside the platform. From phone numbers and email addresses to job titles and favorite colors, lead ads will help you collect any information you want from your potential leads.

Lead ads are superior to website forms for three reasons. First, lead ads were built with the mobile user in mind. Because the forms open directly in Facebook's app, users will never have to leave the app. Instead, they can quickly complete your mobile-friendly form from their devices rather than from a webpage that may load too slowly on a mobile phone. Second, lead ads automatically prefill the forms with users' profile information. This is an amazing feature because it enables a user to accurately complete and submit a form within seconds. Third, most lead ads convert 50 percent better than website forms. This means if you spent $1,000 and generated 1,000 leads with a website form, with that same $1,000 you would be able to generate 2,000 leads with lead ads. Lead ads are undoubtedly a much better use of your money.

Because lead ads are a great way to collect leads, I usually tell all of my clients to have at least 5 percent to 10 percent of their budgets allocated toward lead ads and 80 percent to 90 percent for clients whose campaigns focus solely on generating leads. I recommend that you do the same because all of the data that you collect is yours forever. You can use your leads as recipients for your email, direct mail, Facebook ad, or text messaging campaigns. Remember that, by targeting your leads, you are only showing your ads to targeted users, users who are more likely to care about your product or service.

Creating Lead Ads

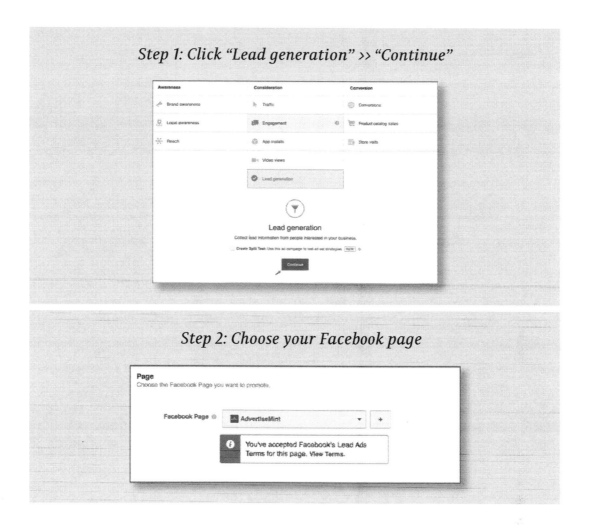

Step 3: Create your target audience

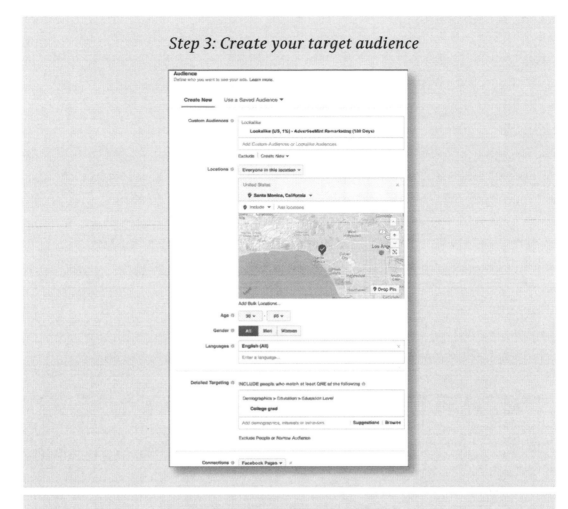

Step 4: Choose your placements

Lead ads are only eligible for Facebook desktop and mobile news feeds and Instagram's feed.

Step 5: Set a budget and schedule

When you set your budget, make sure to optimize for leads rather than for link clicks. Choosing the latter may result in a higher click-through rate. If you want to get the most out of your Facebook ad, always optimize for your goal, which, in this case, is leads.

Step 6: Choose your format

Although your lead ad is eligible for the formats carousel, single image, single video, and slideshow, I recommend sticking with the single image format. Because you don't want to risk losing a lead, and because you want the process to finish as quickly as possible, you want to keep your form simple and easy.

Step 7: Enter text

Write copies that give your audience a clear understanding about your business and your offer. For example, disclose what your customers will get in return (if anything) for their contact information. Will you give them a free ebook? Will you give them email updates about your business? Will you give them notifications about your latest offers?

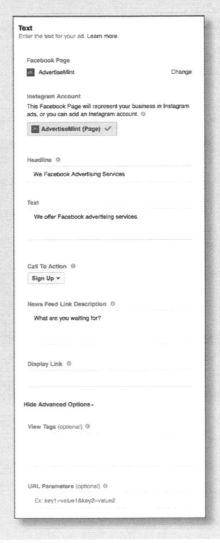

Step 8: Create the form

When you create your form, keep your questions to a minimum. Lengthy forms may dissuade your customers from signing up because they may be reluctant to disclose too much personal information. Only take what you need, which will likely be your customer's full name, email address, and phone number. If you must ask questions on your form, ask multiple choice questions rather than open-ended questions. A convenient process leads to more conversions.

When creating a lead ad, do review the questions you want to ask customers with your legal team as well as carefully study Facebook's lead ad policies and terms of service.

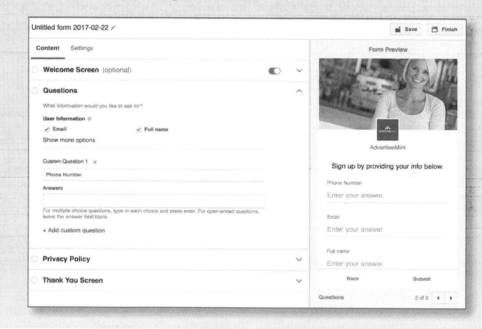

Step 9: You're done

After running your lead ads for a few days, you can then compile the information you obtained into a spreadsheet that you later upload to custom audience. Afterward, use your custom audience to remarket to the customers who responded to your lead ad. I recommend doing this because the customers who responded to your lead ad are most likely to respond to your future ads.

Creating Conditional Answers

Originally, you could only receive multiple-choice and short answers for your lead ads. Recently, however, Facebook updated the lead ad form to allow you to include conditional answers, which automatically change according to the customer's previous response. Examine figure 8.1. As you can see, the first question contains two different answers. In figure 8.1, I answered USA, and, because I gave this answer, the responses to the next question will change accordingly. In figure 8.2, I'm asked which state I live in, and I'm given two states within the United States as the options because, remember, I answered USA to the previous question. When I answer California in figure 8.3, the next question will give me cities from California to choose from.

Figure 8.1 Options will change according to your responses

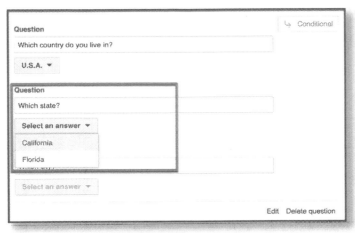

Figure 8.2 Options include states within the United States

Figure 8.3 Options include cities in California

Remember, conditional answers change according to the previous answer you gave. Thus, if I choose the option India rather than USA, the answers will also change. Take a look at figures 8.4 to 8.6. When asked which state I live in, I'm given states in India because I answered India in the previous question. When I'm asked which city, I'm given cities in the state of Haryana.

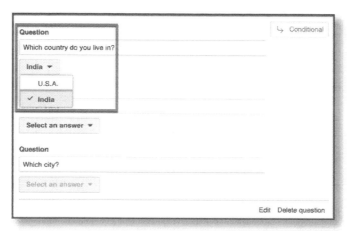

Figure 8.4 Changing response from USA to India

Figure 8.5 Options include states within India

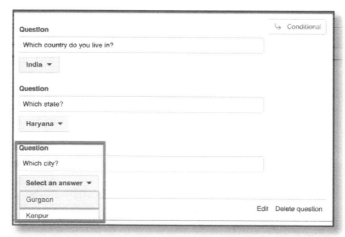

Figure 8.6 Options include cities from the state of Haryana

After seeing the usefulness of lead ad's new conditional answers, you're likely excited to learn how to create one. Creating one can be confusing because you would need to upload a spreadsheet in a particular format, containing all the questions with all the conditional answers. If you don't format it correctly, you can accidentally pair the questions with the wrong answers. Examine figure 8.7, a sample template courtesy of Facebook.

Table 1

U.S.A.	California	Fremont
U.S.A.	California	Menlo Park
U.S.A.	Florida	Orlando
U.S.A.	Florida	Miami
India	Haryana	Gurgaon
India	Haryana	Kanpur
India	Maharashtra	Mumbai
India	Maharashtra	Pune

Figure 8.7 A sample template courtesy of Facebook

In the first column, I have the answers to the first question, "Which country do you live live in?" For the second column, I have answers to the second question, and for the third column, I have answers to the third question. Notice that the answers to the first question in the first column are entered multiple times: there are three entries for USA and four for India. That's because you need to enter each of the first answers with each of the first and second answers. USA needs to be entered three times in the first column because you have to enter

California once to give the answer for Menlo Park and you need to enter Florida twice for the options Orlando and Miami. It's important that you plan your questions and answers before creating the spreadsheet to ensure that you know exactly how to format it. Once you've created your spreadsheet, you can then upload it to your lead ad form.

How to Create Conditional Answers

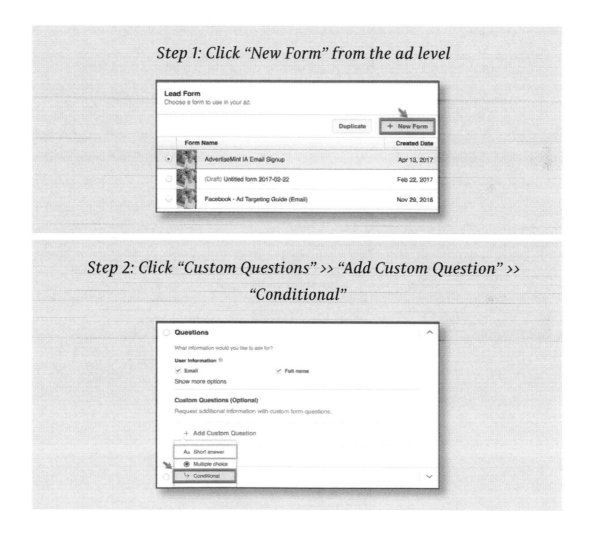

Step 1: Click "New Form" from the ad level

Step 2: Click "Custom Questions" >> "Add Custom Question" >> "Conditional"

Step 3: Upload spreadsheet

Step 4: Write the questions

When you write the questions, make sure that each question is worded in a way that is applicable to all of the possible answers.

Step 5: You're done

After you've created your form, you can submit the lead ad to Facebook for approval.

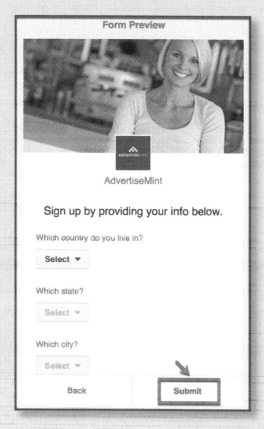

Dynamic Product Ads

Imagine an ad that allows you to target customers at all stages of the sales funnel, an ad that allows you to simultaneously feature multiple products in one creative and products your customers viewed, placed in their cart, or purchased. That ad you imagined is not a fictional product. In fact, it's an ad called a dynamic product ad. Unlike regular single image and video ads, dynamic product ads, which debuted in 2015, are ads that advertise products straight from your product catalog, changing according to the current sales-funnel stage your customers are in.

How does Facebook know which products to show to which customers in which stages of the sales funnel? Facebook uses the Facebook pixel to track the website pages your customers visited (e.g., product catalog or checkout), and based on its findings, it will serve a relevant product to that customer. For example, if your customer browsed through your collection of fur coats, your ad will advertise the fur coats she looked at. If your customer added a fur coat in her cart but did not make a purchase, your ad will remind your customer to finalize her purchase *featuring that exact product*. Dynamic ads are great tools that push interested customers to convert.

Dynamic product ads, if the carousel format is chosen, contain up to ten images and videos that customers can scroll through. They can also feature one relevant product to customers in specific stages of the sales funnel using the single image ad format. With dynamic product ads, you can promote all of your products without having to configure each individual ad, set up your campaigns once and continually reach people with the right product at the right time, reach people with ads on any device they use, and show people ads for products they are interested in to increase the likelihood that they will make a purchase. To create dynamic ads, you must have the items listed below. If you don't have these items, you cannot create dynamic product ads:

· An online product catalog. You can use the existing catalog you use with other online shopping portals. The product catalog you create on Facebook must have a product ID, name, description, landing page URL, image URL, and availability.

· The Facebook pixel. The pixel is an essential element of your dynamic ad because its trackings help you advertise relevant products your customers already expressed interest in.

If you want to promote relevant products from your catalog to interested customers, then you should choose promote a product catalog as your objective and create a dynamic ad. The process of creating a dynamic product ad is slightly different from the process of creating your regular single video or image ad. For one, you can only use the product catalog sales objective.

Creating Dynamic Product Ads

Step 2: Choose your product set and audience

Choose the product you want to feature in your ad. Next, choose the audience to whom you want to target the ad. You can choose to target your ad to people who have viewed or added your products to their carts but did not purchase, have viewed a specific product set in a specific amount of time, or have purchased from the product set in a specific amount of time, or you can target a custom audience of users who interacted with your products.

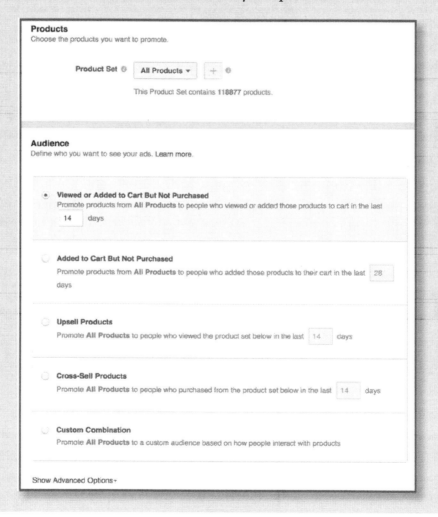

Step 3: Choose your placement

Placements

Show your ads to the right people in the right places.

○ **Automatic Placements (Recommended)**

Your ads will automatically be shown to your audience in the places they're likely to perform best. For this objective, placements may include Facebook, Instagram and Audience Network. **Learn more.**

● **Edit Placements**

Removing placements may reduce the number of people you reach and may make it less likely that you'll meet your goals. **Learn more.**

Step 4: Set your budget and schedule

Budget & Schedule

Define how much you'd like to spend, and when you'd like your ads to appear. **Learn more.**

Budget ⓘ | Daily Budget ▼ | $100.00 |

$100.00 USD

Actual amount spent daily may vary. ⓘ

Schedule ⓘ   ● Run my ad set continuously starting today

○ Set a start and end date

You'll spend no more than **$700.00** per week.

Step 5: Choose your optimization

Choose how you want Facebook to optimize your ad for delivery. If you don't choose carefully, Facebook won't deliver your ads, and your ads will fail. You have three options to choose from: link clicks, impressions, and conversion events. If you choose link clicks, Facebook will show your ads to those who will most likely click on your ad. If you choose impressions, Facebook will show your ads to as many people as possible. If you choose conversion events, Facebook will deliver your ads to those who are more likely to take action when they see a product from your catalog.

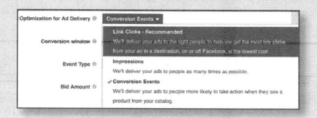

For dynamic product ads, the two popular options are impressions and conversion events. Your choice between these two options depends on your amount of website traffic. If you have a small product catalog and little website traffic, then you should choose impressions. If you have a lot of products and website traffic, then you should choose conversion events. It is necessary that you have a lot of website traffic when choosing conversion events because Facebook requires that you have at least twenty-five conversions a week for it to gather enough data to optimize for conversion events. If you don't have enough conversions for the conversion events optimization, Facebook won't have enough data to know to whom to show your ad, and your ad won't deliver.

Step 6: Choose your conversion window

By choosing a conversion window, or the amount of time between someone clicking or viewing your ad and completing an action you've defined as a conversion event, you're choosing whether Facebook should collect one day or seven days' worth of conversion data when determining who should see your ad. Let's say you chose a one-day conversion window.

Once a customer clicks on your ad, Facebook will track whatever that person is doing on your website for twenty-four hours, whether that action is viewing other products, adding to a cart, or purchasing. After twenty-four hours, Facebook will collect that data to determine who to show your ad to. Conversely, if you chose a seven-day conversion window, Facebook will track that person's actions for seven days. The seven-day window gives Facebook the chance to track more actions from the customer, so it is likely that it will create more useful data to look at.

Although the longer conversion window is recommended for all businesses, your choice should depend on the size of your business and the amount of website traffic you receive. If you're a small business with little website traffic and only a few people interacting with your products, then you should choose the seven-day conversion window. If you own a bigger business and a website with a lot of traffic, then you can choose a one-day conversion window.

Step 7: Choose event type

Conversion events describe a variety of different actions, such as adding to a cart, purchasing, or completing registration. By choosing an event type, you're defining what you consider as a conversion. For dynamic product ads, you can choose to define your conversion event as an add to cart, a purchase, a complete registration, an initial checkout, or a search. In the example below, I defined my conversion event as a purchase. By doing so, Facebook will optimize my Facebook ad by delivering it to those who will most likely make a purchase.

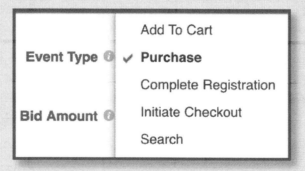

Step 8: Connect your pages

Step 9: Choose your format

You can choose a carousel ad or a single image ad format. When you choose the carousel format, your ad will feature up to ten images of products that your customers viewed, placed in their carts, or purchased and products that are closely related to products your customer bought. When you choose a single image ad format, your ad will feature only one product that your customers either viewed or added to their carts. When deciding which of these two ad formats to use, ask yourself this question: Do you want to encourage your customers to buy more products or do you want them to buy only the product they have previously viewed or added to their carts? If you want the former, then use the carousel format. If the latter is the case, then use the single image format. Although both are valuable, I usually use the carousel format because it encourages customers to scroll through the carousel cards, consequently increasing the ad's relevancy score. Additionally, the carousel format for dynamic product ads is usually cheaper than the single image format.

Step 10: Add links, copies, pixel tracking, and CTA buttons

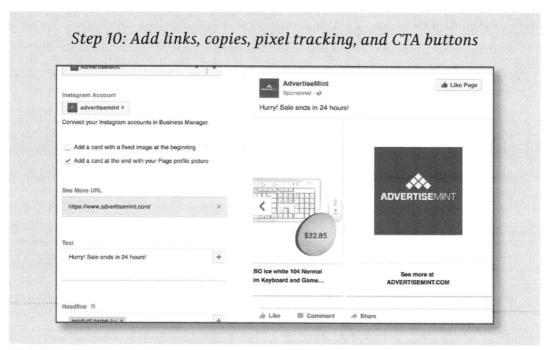

Step 11: You're done

Slideshow Ads

Slideshow ads are a great tool for two reasons. First, they work especially well in countries that have slow connections speeds. In fact, Facebook created the slideshow format for that exact purpose, to create visually appealing ads that do not require fast internet connectivity. While more complex ads such as video and canvas ads load slowly in those areas, slideshows load quickly and easily because they are lightweight, containing only basic transitions and movements between the slides. Second, slideshow ads are a great alternative to video ads, especially for those small companies that do not have the money or the resources to create video ads. This ad format, by flashing slide after slide of images to create a story in a very flip-book-esque fashion, has the illusion of a video. Although perfect for smaller companies with smaller budgets, slideshow ads have also been favored by large companies such as Unilever and Stance.

Creating a Slideshow Ad

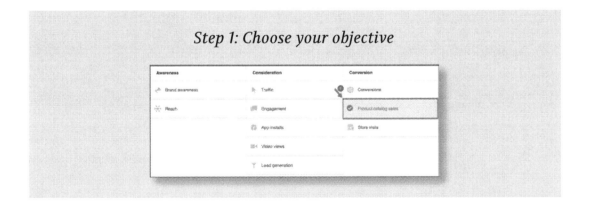

Step 1: Choose your objective

Step 2: Choose your audience

Step 3: Choose your placement

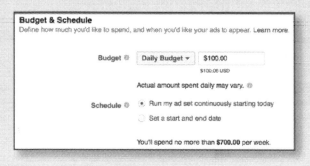

Step 4: Choose your budget and schedule

Step 5: Connect your pages

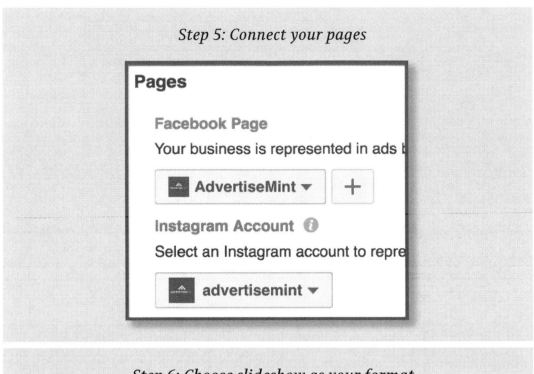

Step 6: Choose slideshow as your format

Step 7: Choose your media

When creating your slideshow, you can choose photos only (you can include up to ten), a combination of photos and videos, or text only. If you choose to upload a video, you will have the option to add captions. After choosing your media, you must also choose your aspect ratio, image duration (how long you want your image to appear in the slide), transition type, and music.

If you want to upload music to your slideshow, you must use one of the formats WAV, MP3, M4A, FLAC, and OGG. Additionally, you must have all legal rights necessary to use a song. Songs that you licensed for use are allowed, whereas songs you purchased or downloaded are not. If you don't have an audio track, you can use the free music from Facebook's library.

Step 8: Add your text, URL, and pixel tracking

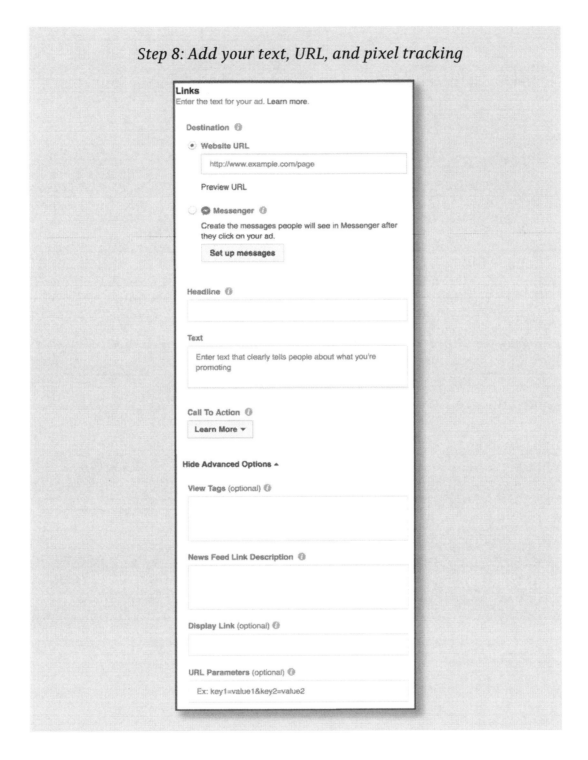

Canvas Ads

Canvas ads are a great way to create a full immersive experience on mobile devices. A canvas ad will appear as a regular ad on news feed with a small circle at the bottom of the ad. When users click on the small circle, the ad will open, taking up the entire screen on a mobile phone. Canvas ads are like Legos: you can combine and stack different elements such as texts, videos, images, carousels, and buttons on top of each other.

Creating Canvas Ads Using a Template (the Easier Option)

Step 1: From the ad level, choose a format >> click "Add a full-screen experience" >> choose a template

You have three temples to choose from. One will help you get new customers (much like a lead ad), one will help you showcase your business (much like the brand awareness objective), and one will help you sell products (much like a dynamic product ad).

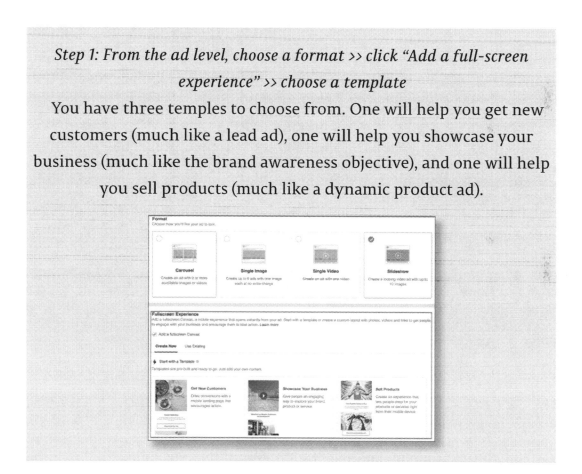

Step 2: Add your media, text, CTA button, and website URL

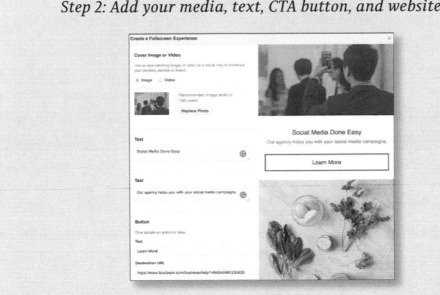

Step 3: Preview and submit

Once you send a preview to your phone, Facebook will send you a notification on your Facebook app. After you're satisfied with the preview, you can then submit the ad to Facebook for approval.

Creating Canvas Ads Using the Advanced Canvas Builder (the Harder Option)

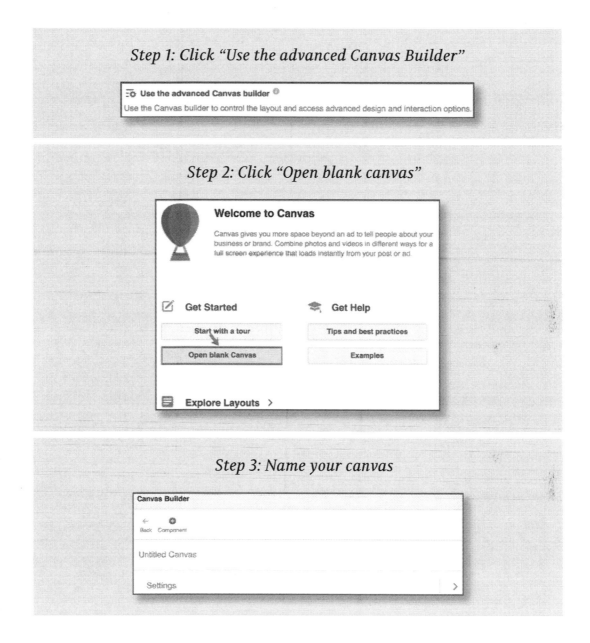

Step 4: Update settings

You can choose between three themes: light, dark, and custom. After you've chosen your theme, you can enable swipe to open, a feature that, appearing on the last component of your canvas ad, links to a website or an app.

Step 5: Add components

You can add several components:

- **Header:** This image will appear at the top of your canvas ad and will remain there as users scroll down. For best results, images should be 882 x 66 pixels.

- **Text block:** This will appear underneath your header. You can modify your text's font, size, color, alignment, and spacing. You can also modify the cell padding and background color.

- **Photo:** This will appear under your header and text block. Upload a photo with a width of 1080 pixels for the best results. When adding a photo, you can include a destination URL in the http:// format, which is where users will be taken if they click on the image. You can also modify the image padding and image format:
  - Fit to width (linkable): This takes up the width of the canvas ad. A URL link can be added.
  - Fit to width (tap to expand): This expands to full screen when users tap the image. They can also zoom out of the image.
  - Fit to height (tilt to pan): An image can fit cell phone screens both vertically and horizontally when people tilt their devices to rotate the image from side to side.

- **Video:** This will appear under your header and text block. Keep your videos (.mp4 or .mov) under two minutes and use captions. Video format options: fit to width and fit to height.

- **Button:** This will appear under your photo or video. It allows you to direct users to a web page or app store using a URL in the http:// format. You can edit the button's color, style (border or fill), font, font size, font color, padding, positioning, and background.

- **Carousel:** You can upload up to ten images. If images are not the same size, they will be cropped to match your first image. Each image must have a URL in the http:// format. You can edit the carousel's component padding and layout to linkable fit to width and tiltable fit to height.

- **Product sets:** You can upload a product catalog and display up to fifty products.

- **Store locator:** You can direct people nearby to your location.

Step 6: Save, preview, share, and submit

Once you complete your canvas ad, you must first save it before you can preview, share, or submit the ad. The options to save, preview, share, and submit are located on the top bar of the editor box. You can edit your canvas ad by previewing it.

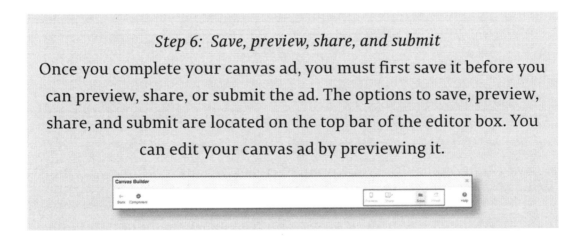

Collection Ads

A prospective buyer scrolls through his news feed and stops at a video ad, which automatically plays. Eyes gleaming with avarice, he watches the Adidas Pure Boost ZG Trainer Shoes—dark, beautiful, and sleek—float before him. He wants to have them now, but the video doesn't link to the website. In fact, if he wants to buy the shoes, he'd have to hunt them down. He'd have to go to Google and search for them. The moment passes. With a shrug he continues scrolling through his news feed, completely forgetting the shoes he, for a split second, coveted.

That's how quickly a customer can be lost. It's a matter of convenience, and it's up to you to provide it.

Although video ads are great for attracting and sustaining attention, they're not so great with helping customers find the item they want to buy. Fortunately, Facebook solved that predicament by launching an enhanced version of video ads, a version that allows customers to find and buy the product featured in the video. This new video ad is called collections. Collection ads allow you to attach multiple product images to the bottom of a video or image ad in a news feed. For example, if your video ad features the Pure Boost ZG Trainer Shoes, you can attach images of those shoes to the bottom of the ad. Once customers click on the image, they will be taken to a product catalog Facebook hosts. Note, however, that although customers can access the catalog through the platform, they cannot make a purchase right then and there. Rather, once they click, they will be taken to your website, where they can then make their purchase.

When you create a collection ad, you're combining the steps of creating a video ad and a dynamic product ad. I have discussed in detail the processes involved in the section "Dynamic Product Ads"; I urge you to review that section before continuing with this one.

Creating Collection Ads

Step 1: Choose conversions or traffic as your objective

Step 2: Choose your conversion pixel

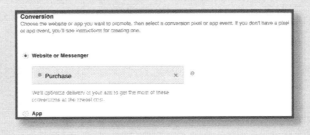

Step 3: Choose your audience

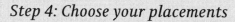

Step 4: Choose your placements

Step 5: Set your budget and schedule

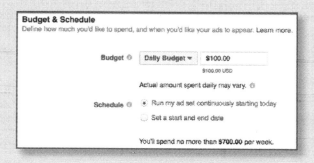

Step 6: Connect your pages

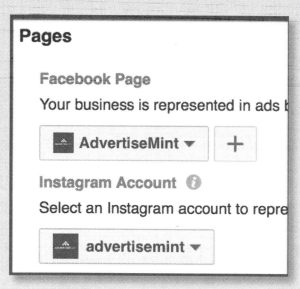

Step 7: Choose the collection format

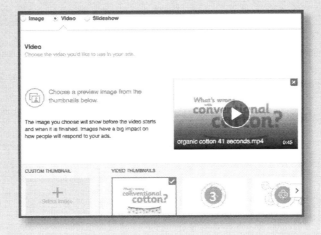

Step 8: Upload your media

When you upload your video, you will have to choose your video thumbnail, or the image that appears before your video starts and when it finishes. I suggest using a thumbnail that provides a sneak peek of the video's message, sparks intrigue, and compels your audience to click. In the example below, I capture the attention of eco-friendly, concerned mothers by choosing a thumbnail that gives them a surprising and scary fact about children's underwear.

Step 9: Add your text, product catalog, product set, URL, and pixel tracking

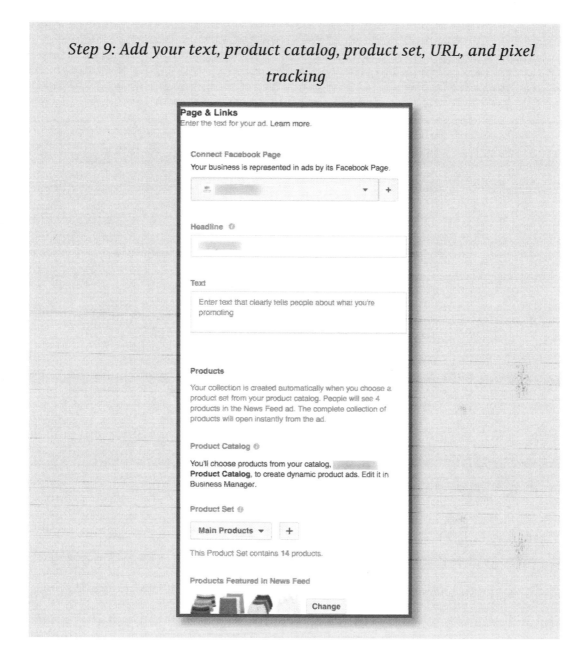

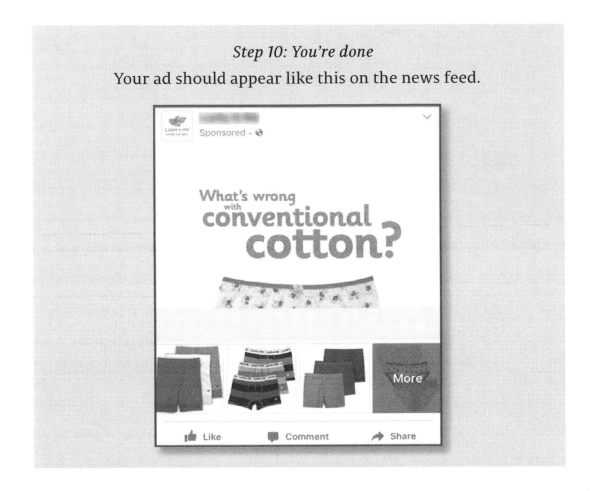

Step 10: You're done

Your ad should appear like this on the news feed.

App Install Ads

App install ads allow you to advertise your apps to users. Once users click your ad, they will be redirected to the app store from which they can install your ad. To create app install ads, you must first connect your app to the Facebook for Developers website and to Business Manager. Only then will you be able to use your app to create app install ads.

Linking Your App to a Facebook Developers Account

Step 1: Download the Facebook SDK into your app

· SDK for iOS: https://developers.facebook.com/docs/ios/

· SDK for Android:

Step 2: Go to developers.facebook.com >> click "My Apps" >> "Add a New App"

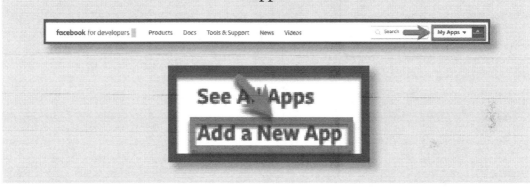

Step 3: Create a new app ID >> select "Create App ID"

Step 4: Complete the captcha

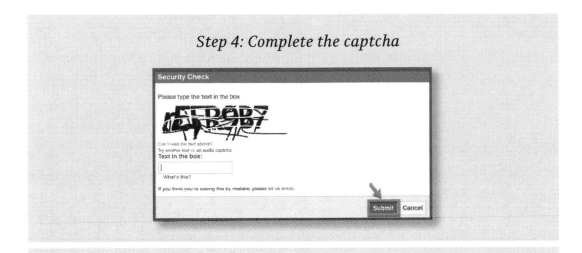

Step 5: Link your app ID and app secret to SDK >> fill out information

Step 6: Set settings

Assign any advanced settings. It's important that you set up your domains, app page, Business Manager, and any authorized advertising accounts.

Step 7: Assign roles

Enter the name or username of the person you would like to add.
Only admins can create app install ads for your app.

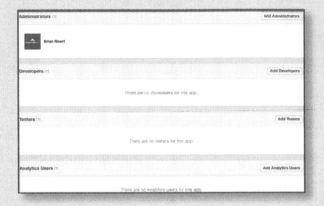

Step 8: Click "App Review" >> Make [App Name] Public >> Slide to Yes

Linking App through Business Manager

The next step you need to do is to link your app to Business Manager.

Step 1: Go to business settings >> select the apps icon

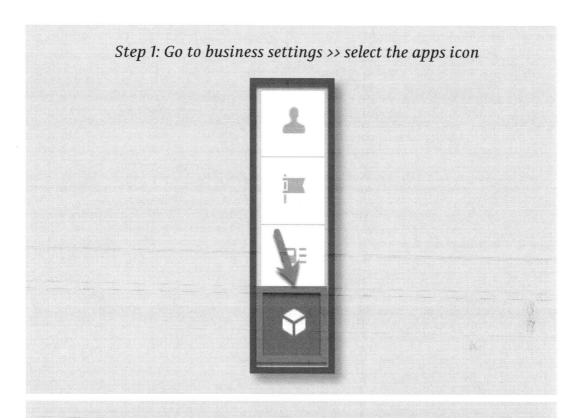

Step 2: Select "Add New Apps" >> "Add an App"

If you own the app, select "Add an App." If you don't own the app, select "Request Access to an App."

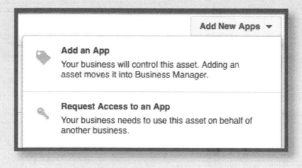

Step 3: Enter app ID >> click "Add App"

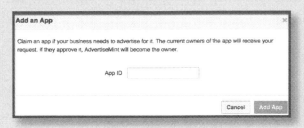

Step 4: Click "Assign Ad Accounts" >> choose ad account >> click "Save Changes"

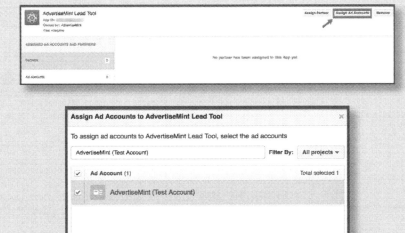

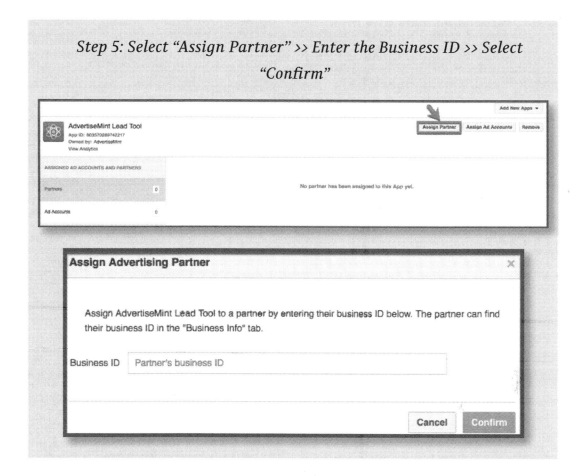

Step 5: Select "Assign Partner" >> Enter the Business ID >> Select "Confirm"

Once you've connected your app to the SDK and to Business Manager, it will be available for attachment when creating app install ads.

Creating an app install ad

Step 1: Choose the objective "app installs"

App installs is the only objective eligible for the app install ad. If you don't choose this objective, you won't be able to create app install ads.

Step 2: Choose an app to promote

Enter your app's URL.

Step 3: Upload a catalog (optional)

This optional feature will automatically show users an item that they will most likely purchase.

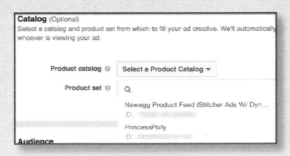

Step 4: Create your audience

Step 5: Select your mobile devices and operating systems

Based on the type of app you have, Facebook should automatically choose the devices and operating systems the app is compatible with. You shouldn't worry about this section unless you want to specify the device versions you want your ad to appear in or unless you want your ad to appear to devices that are only connected to Wi-Fi.

Step 6: Choose your budget and schedule

Budget & Schedule
Define how much you'd like to spend, and when you'd like your ads to appear. Learn more.

Budget Daily Budget $ $40.00
$40.00 USD

Actual amount spent daily may vary.

Schedule • Run my ad set continuously starting today
 ○ Set a start and end date

You'll spend no more than $280.00 per week.

Step 7: Choose your optimization

I highly recommend optimizing for app installs. As always, you should optimize for the goal that you want to achieve, which, in this case, is app installs.

Step 8: Add more specifications

Choose your conversion window, bid amount, charges, ad schedule, and delivery type. Remember that your conversion window is the amount of time between someone clicking or viewing your ad and completing an action you've defined as a conversion event, such as purchases. If you choose a one-day conversion window, Facebook will track your customer's actions on your website for 24 hours, whether that action is viewing other products, adding to cart, or purchasing.

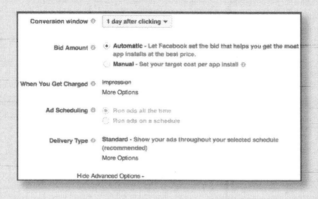

Step 9: Choose your Facebook and Instagram pages

Step 10: Choose your format

Step 11: Choose your image

Although you can upload an image for your ad, Facebook will automatically upload an image you used as the preview image for the app.

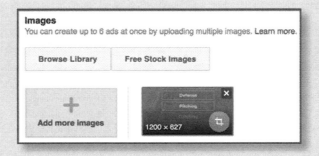

Step 12: Add your text

Don't forget to check the option that allows you to track all conversions from your Facebook pixel.

Step 13: You're done

You should be able to see a preview of your ad. Once you're done, you can send your ad to Facebook.

Store Visits Ads

In chapter 5, I taught you how to set your main business page in Business Manager. (If you haven't read that chapter, I urge you to do so before continuing with this section.) I also explained that you must set your business location to create store visits ads. If you recall, store visits ads are ads that direct users to your nearest physical location. For example, if you saw a store visits ad from McDonald's, and you clicked on the "Get Directions" CTA, the ad will give you directions to a McDonald's near you. However, in order for Facebook to locate all of your physical locations on a map, you must first enable business location. If you don't do this, you won't be able to create store visits ads.

Creating Store Visits Ads

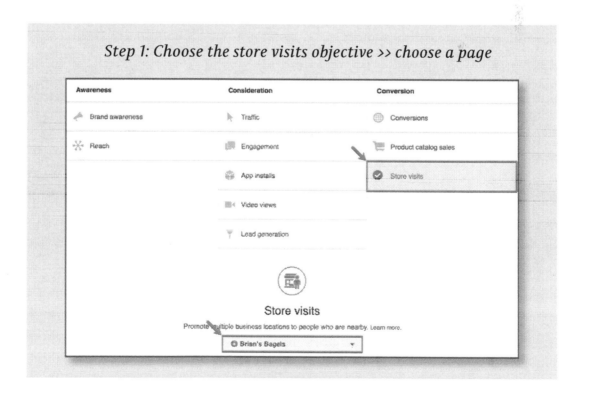

Step 2: Select business locations and radius

You must select the business locations you want included in your ad. You can add locations by entering your locations' zip codes, store numbers, or designated market areas (DMA). You will also be able to set your radius size, or the area around each of your business locations that you want to target users in. You have two choices for your radius size: you can set it to audience or to distance. If you choose audience, Facebook will target ads to the number of people you want to reach. If you choose distance, Facebook will target users within the radius that you choose.

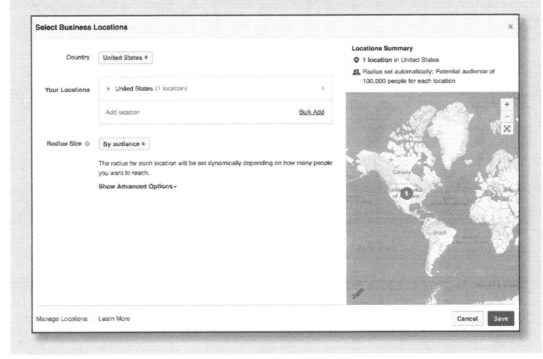

Step 3: Choose your placements

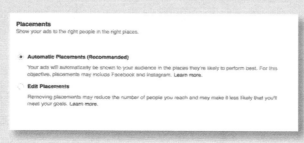

Step 4: Choose your budget and schedule

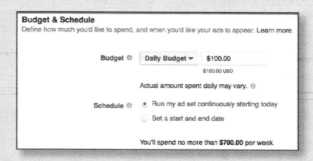

Step 5: Choose your format

Step 6: Choose your media

Step 7: Add your texts, pages, links, CTAs, and pixel tracking

In this section, along with adding your texts, CTAs, and pixel tracking, you will also be able to choose your ad's voice, for which you have two options: main page and local pages. If you choose the main page, your ad will only contain your business's name. If you choose local pages, your ad will contain both your business's name and it's city location.

In this section, you will also choose from among a page, a website URL, or a store locator destination. In the first option, the ad, once clicked, will send users to your business's Facebook page. In the second option, they will be redirected to your business's URL. If the third option, they will be directed to a map where they can find your business's location. Once you finish the last step, you will be able to submit your ad to Facebook for approval.

Text

Enter the text for your ad. **Learn more.**

Ad Voice ⓘ

Ads will be delivered for locations with the following options on Facebook placements

- Main Page name
- Clicks on ad will take people to Main Page
- Likes and comments will appear on the post
- Directions, phone numbers, etc. will be for Local Page

Offers Ads

Offer ads, the digital versions of coupons, include discount codes that customers can use at checkout. If you want to create an offer ad, you must select the conversion or traffic objective because those are the objectives eligible for offers.

Creating Offers Ads

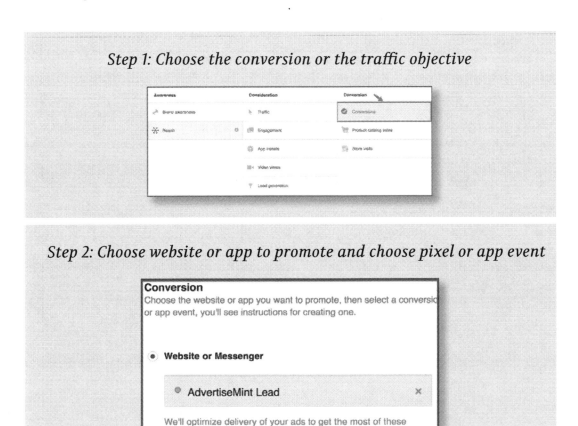

Step 1: Choose the conversion or the traffic objective

Step 2: Choose website or app to promote and choose pixel or app event

Step 3: Create your offer

- **Create offer title**

- **Add offer details**

- **Set offer schedule**

- **Set redemption location:** You can allow code redemption online or in store. If online, you must add the website URL where users can redeem your offer.

- **Create promo code:** You can exclude a promo code, add one code, or add unique codes. If you add one code, multiple users will be able to use the one code you created. If you add unique codes, each user will have different codes to use. For unique codes, you must download a CSV file with all the codes listed.

- **Enter the number of offers you want to give**

- **Set advanced options (optional):** You can prevent people from sharing the coupon, and you can upload your offers' terms and conditions.

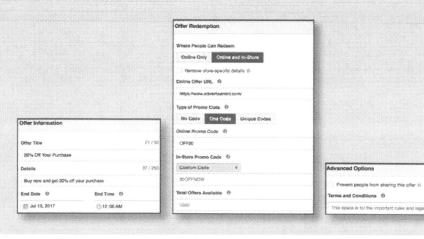

Step 4: Add target audience

Step 5: Choose placements

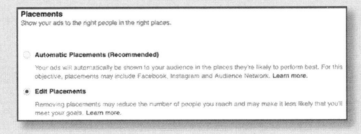

Step 6: Set budget and schedule

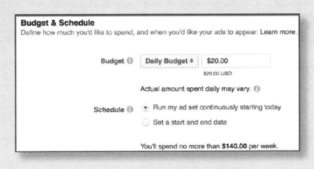

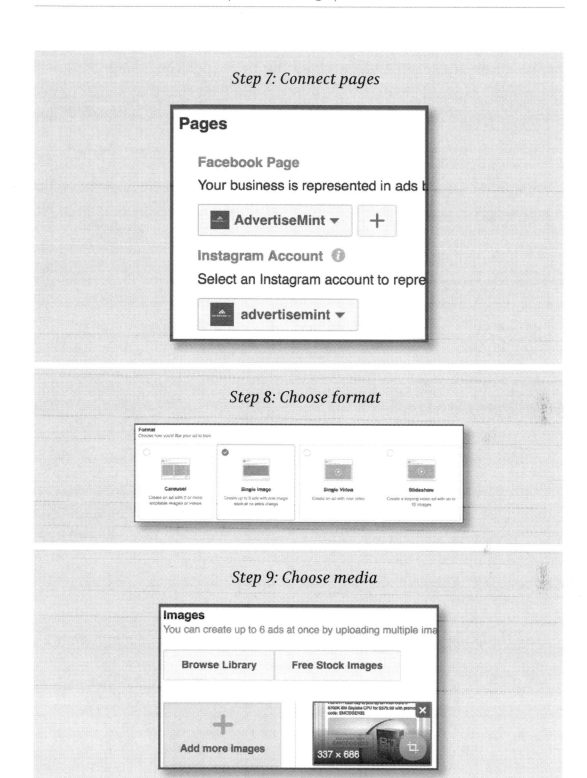

Step 7: Connect pages

Step 8: Choose format

Step 9: Choose media

Step 10: Add text

Creative

Preview the image and text from your offer claim. **Learn more.**

Text

Enter text that clearly tells people about what you're promoting

CHAPTER 9: FACEBOOK AD GUIDELINES AND POLICIES

Before your Instagram and Facebook ads can be published for the world to see, they must first abide by Facebook's ad policies. When you submit your ads for approval, Facebook will review them to ensure they aren't violating its policies. It will check your ads' image, text, targeting, positioning, and landing page. Facebook will review your ads within twenty-four hours, although some ads may take longer. After the review process, Facebook will send you an email notification stating whether your ads were approved.

If your ads don't abide by Facebook's policies, they will be rejected. If your ads were rejected, you must edit them according to Facebook's disapproval details. If you think your ads were falsely disapproved, you can appeal the decision.[10] To avoid delays and confusion, it's important that you carefully study Facebook's advertising policies, which I have included in this chapter. You can also read Facebook's policies online.[11]

---

10   Appeal at https://www.facebook.com/help/contact/1582364792025146/.

11   Visit Facebook's policy online at https://www.facebook.com/policies/ads/.

Prohibited Content

1. Community Standards

Ads must not violate our Community Standards. Ads on Instagram must not violate the Instagram Community Guidelines.

2. Illegal Products or Services

Ads must not constitute, facilitate, or promote illegal products, services, or activities. Ads targeted to minors must not promote products, services, or content that are inappropriate, illegal, or unsafe or that exploit, mislead, or exert undue pressure on the age groups targeted.

3. Discriminatory Practices

Ads must not discriminate or encourage discrimination against people based on personal attributes such as race, ethnicity, color, national origin, religion, age, sex, sexual orientation, gender identity, family status, disability, or medical or genetic condition.

4. Tobacco Products

Ads must not promote the sale or use of tobacco products and related paraphernalia.

5. Drugs and Drug-Related Products

Ads must not promote the sale or use of illegal, prescription, or recreational drugs.

6. Unsafe Supplements

Ads must not promote the sale or use of unsafe supplements, as determined by Facebook in its sole discretion.

7. Weapons, Ammunition, or Explosives

Ads must not promote the sale or use of weapons, ammunition, or explosives.

8. Adult Products or Services

Ads must not promote the sale or use of adult products or services, except for ads for family planning and contraception. Ads for contraceptives must focus on the contraceptive features of the product, and not on sexual pleasure or sexual enhancement, and it must target people 18 years or older.

9. Adult Content

Ads must not contain adult content. This includes nudity, depictions of people in explicit or suggestive positions, or activities that are overly suggestive or sexually provocative.

10. Third-Party Infringement

Ads must not contain content that infringes upon or violates the rights of any third party, including copyright, trademark, privacy, publicity, or other personal or proprietary rights.

11. Sensational Content

Ads must not contain shocking, sensational, disrespectful, or excessively violent content.

12. Personal Attributes

Ads must not contain content that asserts or implies personal attributes. This includes direct or indirect assertions or implications about a person's race, ethnic origin, religion, beliefs, age, sexual orientation or practices, gender identity, disability, medical condition (including physical or mental health), financial status, membership in a trade union, criminal record, or name.

13. Misleading or False Content

Ads must not contain deceptive, false, or misleading content, including deceptive claims, offers, or business practices.

14. Controversial Content

Ads must not contain content that exploits controversial political or social issues for commercial purposes.

15. Non-Functional Landing Page

Ads must not direct people to non-functional landing pages. This includes landing page content that interferes with a person's ability to navigate away from the page.

16. Surveillance Equipment

Ads may not promote the sale of spy cams, mobile phone trackers, or other hidden surveillance equipment.

17. Grammar and Profanity

Ads must not contain profanity or bad grammar and punctuation. Symbols, numbers, and letters must be used properly.

18. Nonexistent Functionality

Ads must not contain images that portray nonexistent functionality.

19. Personal Health

Ads must not contain before-and-after images or images that contain unexpected or unlikely results. Ads must not imply or attempt to generate negative self-perception in order to promote diet, weight loss, or other health-related products. Ads for health, fitness, or weight loss products must target people 18 years or older.

20. Payday or Cash Advance Loans

Ads must not promote payday loans, paycheck advances, or any other short-term loan intended to cover someone's expenses until their next payday.

21. Multilevel Marketing

Ads promoting income opportunities must fully describe the associated product or business model and must not promote business models offering quick compensation for little investment, including multilevel marketing opportunities.

22. Penny Auctions

Ads may not promote penny auctions, bidding fee auctions, or other similar business models.

23. Counterfeit Documents

Ads may not promote fake documents, such as counterfeit degrees, passports, or immigration papers.

The Complete Guide to Facebook Advertising

24. Low-Quality or Disruptive Content

Ads must not lead to external landing pages that provide an unexpected or disruptive experience. This includes misleading ad positioning, such as overly sensationalized headlines, and landing pages with minimal original, unrelated, or low-quality content.

25. Spyware or Malware

Ads must not contain spyware, malware, or any software that results in an unexpected or deceptive experience. This includes links to sites containing these products.

26. Automatic Animation

Ads must not contain audio or flash animation that plays automatically without a person's interaction or expands within Facebook after someone clicks on the ad.

27. Unauthorized Streaming Devices

Ads must not promote products or items that facilitate or encourage unauthorized access to digital media.

Restricted Content

1. Alcohol

Ads that promote or reference alcohol must comply with all applicable local laws, required or established industry codes, guidelines, licenses, and approvals. Ads must include age and country targeting criteria consistent with Facebook's targeting guidelines and applicable local laws. Note that ads promoting or referencing alcohol are prohibited in some countries, including but not limited to Afghanistan, Brunei, Bangladesh, Egypt, Gambia, Kuwait, Libya, Norway, Pakistan, Russia, Saudi Arabia, Turkey, United Arab Emirates, and Yemen.

2. Dating

Ads for online dating services are only allowed with prior written permission. These must adhere to the dating targeting requirements and our dating quality guidelines. In order to be a registered dating partner, you must fill out our dating advertiser application to begin your application process.[12]

3. Real Money Gambling

Ads that promote or facilitate online real money gambling, real money games of skill, or real money lotteries, including online real money casino, sports books, bingo, or poker, are only allowed with prior written permission. Authorized gambling, games of skill or lottery ads must target people 18 years or older who are in jurisdictions for which permission has been granted.

---

12   Access application at https://www.facebook.com/help/contact/176964042711831.

4. State Lotteries

Lotteries run by government entities may advertise on Facebook provided the ads are targeted in accordance with applicable law in the jurisdiction in which the ads will be served and only target people in the jurisdiction in which the lottery is available.

5. Online Pharmacies

Ads must not promote the sale of prescription pharmaceuticals. Ads for online and offline pharmacies are only permitted with prior written permission.

6. Supplements

Ads that promote acceptable dietary and herbal supplements may only target people who are at least 18 years of age.

7. Subscription Services

Ads for subscription services, or ads that promote products or services that include negative options, automatic renewal, free-to-pay conversion billing products, or mobile marketing, are subject to our subscription services requirements.

8. Financial Services

Ads promoting credit card applications or financial services with accredited institutions must clearly provide sufficient disclosure regarding associated fees, including APR percentages transaction fees within the ad's landing page. Ads promoting loans or insurance services must not directly request the input of a person's financial information, including credit card information.

9. Branded Content

Ads promoting branded content must tag the featured third-party product, brand, or business partner using the branded content tool. Branded content within ads is defined as a creator's or publisher's content that features or is influenced by a business partner for an exchange of value. When promoting branded content integrations, advertisers must use the branded content tool.

10. Student Loan Services

Ads promoting student loan services must target people 18 years or older. Ads must not promote misleading or deceptive services related to student loan consolidation, forgiveness, or refinancing.

Video Ads

Video ads and other dynamic ad types must comply with all of the rules listed in these advertising policies, including the Community Standards, as well as the policies below:

1. Disruptive Content

Videos and other similar ad types must not use overly disruptive tactics, such as flashing screens.

2. Entertainment-Related Restrictions

Ads for movie trailers, TV shows, video game trailers, and other similar content intended for mature audiences are only allowed with prior written permission from Facebook and must target people who are 18 years or older. Excessive depictions of the following content within these ads are not allowed:

- Drugs and alcohol use

- Adult content

- Profanity

- Violence and gore

Targeting

1. You must not use targeting options to discriminate against, harass, provoke, or disparage users or to engage in predatory advertising practices.

2. If you target your ads to custom audiences, you must comply with the applicable terms when creating an audience.

Positioning

1. Relevance

All ad components, including any text, images, or other media, must be relevant and appropriate to the product or service being offered and to the audience viewing the ad.

2. Accuracy

Ads must clearly represent the company, product, service, or brand that is being advertised.

3. Related Landing Pages

The products and services promoted in an ad's text must match those promoted on the landing page, and the destination site must not offer or link to any prohibited product or service.

Text in Images

Our policies previously prohibited ads with text that covered more than 20% of an ad's image. We've recently implemented a new solution that allows ads with greater than 20% text to run, but with less or no delivery.

Lead Ads

Advertisers must not create lead ads questions to request the following types of information without our prior written permission.

1. Account Numbers

Ads must not request account numbers, including frequent flyer numbers, loyalty card numbers, or cable or telephone account numbers without our prior permission.

2. Criminal History

Ads must not request information regarding criminal or arrest history without our prior permission.

3. Financial Information

Ads must not request financial information, including bank account numbers, bank routing numbers, credit or debit card numbers, credit scores, income, net worth, or debt amount without our prior permission.

4. Government-Issued Identifiers

Ads must not request government-issued identifiers, including Social Security numbers, passport numbers, or driver's license numbers without our prior permission.

5. Health Information

Ads must not request health information, including physical health, mental health, medical treatments, medical conditions, or disabilities without our prior permission.

6. Insurance Information

Ads must not request insurance information, including current insurance policy numbers, without our prior permission.

7. Political Affiliation

Ads must not request information regarding political affiliation without our prior permission.

8. Race or Ethnicity

Ads must not request information regarding race or ethnicity without our prior permission.

9. Religion

Ads must not request information regarding religion or philosophical beliefs without our prior permission.

10. Sexual Orientation

Ads must not request information regarding sexual orientation or information about the sexual life of the individual, including what gender(s) the person prefers to date, without our prior permission.

11. Template Questions

Ads must not request the same or substantially similar information that you could use a template question to request.

12. Trade Union Membership

Ads must not request information regarding trade union membership status without our prior permission.

13. Usernames or Passwords

Ads must not request usernames or passwords, including usernames and passwords for existing and new accounts, without our prior permission. If you want to direct people to sign up for an account with your site or service, you should use the clicks to website or website conversions objective when you run your ads.

Use of Our Brand Assets

1. Brand Endorsement

Ads must not imply a Facebook or Instagram endorsement or partnership of any kind or an endorsement by any other Facebook Company.

2. Facebook's Brands

Ads linking to Facebook or Instagram branded content (including pages, groups, events, or sites that use Facebook login) may make limited reference to Facebook or Instagram in ad text for the purpose of clarifying the destination of the ad.

3. Copyrights and Trademarks

All other ads and landing pages must not use our copyrights, trademarks, or any confusingly similar marks, except as expressly permitted by our Brand Usage Guidelines or the Instagram Brand Guidelines or with our prior written permission.

Data Use Restrictions

1. Ensure any ad data collected, received, or derived from your Facebook or Instagram ad ("Facebook advertising data") is only shared with someone acting on your behalf, such as your service provider. You are responsible for ensuring your service providers protect any Facebook advertising data or any other information obtained from us, limit their use of all of that information, and keep it confidential and secure.

2. Don't use Facebook advertising data for any purpose (including retargeting, commingling data across multiple advertisers' campaigns, or allowing piggybacking or redirecting with tags) except when using the data in an aggregate and anonymous basis (unless authorized by Facebook) and when assessing the performance and effectiveness of your Facebook advertising campaigns.

3. Don't use Facebook advertising data, including the targeting criteria for your ad, to build, append to, edit, influence, or augment user profiles, including profiles associated with any mobile device identifier or other unique identifier that identifies any particular user, browser, computer, or device.

4. Don't transfer any Facebook advertising data (including anonymous, aggregate, or derived data) to any ad network, ad exchange, data broker, or other advertising or monetization related service.

Things You Should Know

1. The Advertising Policies apply to (1) ads and commercial content served by or purchased through Facebook, on or off the Facebook services, including ads purchased under AAAA/IAB Standard Terms and Conditions, (2) ads appearing within apps on Facebook, and (3) ads on Instagram. Your use of Facebook's advertising products and services is part of "Facebook" under Facebook's Statement of Rights and Responsibilities (https://www.facebook.com/legal/terms,

the "SRR") and is subject to the SRR. You may be subject to additional terms or guidelines if you use Instagram or certain Facebook advertising-related products or services.

2. Advertisers are responsible for understanding and complying with all applicable laws and regulations. Failure to comply may result in a variety of consequences, including the cancellation of ads you have placed and termination of your account.

3. We do not use sensitive personal data for ad targeting. Topics you choose for targeting your ad don't reflect the personal beliefs, characteristics, or values of the people who use Facebook or Instagram.

4. If you are managing ads on behalf of other advertisers, each advertiser or client must be managed through separate ad accounts. You must not change the advertiser or client associated with an established ad account. Rather, you must set up a new account. You are responsible for ensuring that each advertiser complies with these advertising policies.

5. We reserve the right to reject, approve, or remove any ad for any reason in our sole discretion, including ads that negatively affect our relationship with our users or that promote content, services, or activities contrary to our competitive position, interests, or advertising philosophy.

6. For policies that require prior written permission, Facebook or a Facebook company may grant these permissions.

7. These policies are subject to change at any time without notice.

CHAPTER 10: MANAGING YOUR FACEBOOK PAGE

Creating a Facebook page with the intention of only using it to access Business Manager is a fool's dream. You can't create one and neglect it forever. You have to improve it, build it up, and maintain it. After all, your page will represent all of the ads that appear on Facebook's platforms. Users will be able to see the page associated with your ad, and they will be able to click on the page to visit it. For that reason, it's important that your page be professional, active, and up to date. This chapter is dedicated to managing your Facebook page, from adding page roles, verifications, and followers to leveraging important page tools.

Updating Your Settings

When your page goes live, you must immediately update your settings to fit your business goals. Although there are many preferences you can adjust from your page's settings, most of which you likely won't need to change, I have discussed a few that I believe are the most important. (Remember, you can access your page from the left column of news feed and your page settings on the left side of your page's header.)

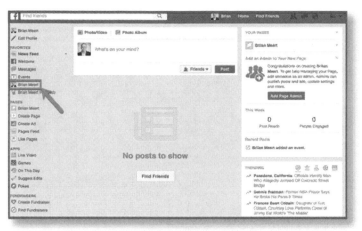

Figure 10.1

Figure 10.2

Assigning Page Roles

If you work with a social media team, this will be the first thing you would want to do. Managing a page alone can be difficult, especially if your page receives a constant flow of comments and messages from hundreds of followers. With a business to manage and a personal life to maintain, you likely have very little time to review and respond to every message, notification, comment, and review. Fortunately, you can assign page roles such as editor, advertiser, admin, and analyst to your team, who can help you manage your page.

Step 1: Click "Page Roles"

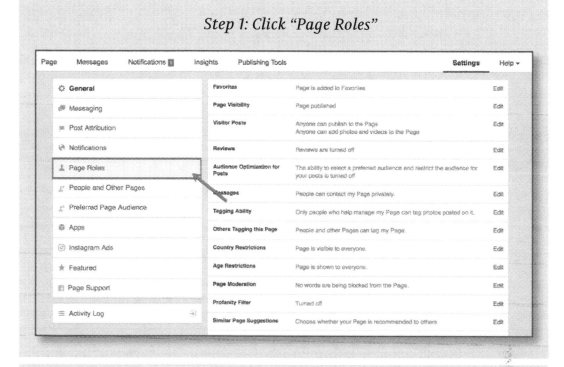

Step 2: Assign role

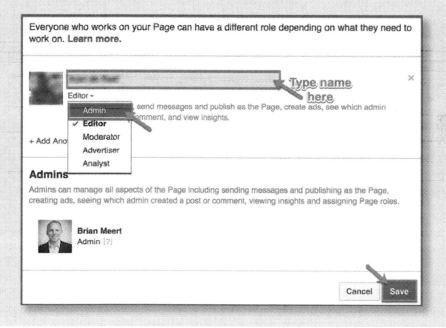

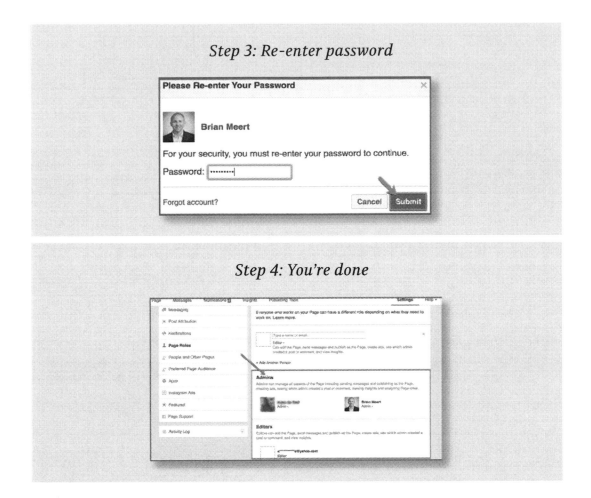

Updating Preferred Audience

If you recall in chapter 3, where I taught you how to create a Facebook page, you learned how to set a preferred audience, or the audience to whom you want Facebook to show your page. As you begin to advertise, however, and as you study more and more of your page insights, you might later find that your audience shifted or a new audience is interested in your business. Fortunately, the preferred audience you chose when you created your page isn't the audience you're stuck with forever—you can change your preferred audience to target the new audience you discovered in your insights.

Step 1: Click "Preferred Page Audience"

Step 2: Click "Edit"

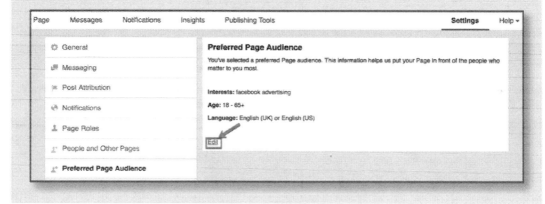

Step 3: Edit preferences >> save

You can edit your audience's geography, age, gender, and language. For example, you can select or exclude any country, state, and city. The more information you provide, the more specific will be your target. Keep in mind, however, that you should not make your preferences too narrow, lest you exclude a good potential audience.

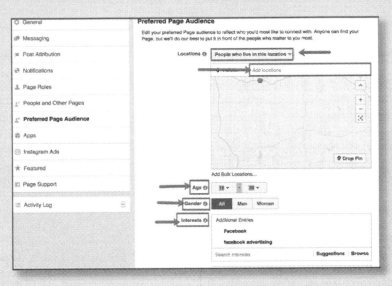

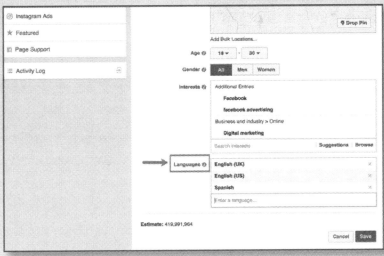

Adding an Instagram Account

If you want to create Instagram ads without connecting your Instagram account to Business Manager, add your Instagram account to your Facebook page that you are an admin or an editor of. Remember, you can't advertise on Instagram without connecting your Instagram account to either your Business Manager or your Facebook page.

Step 1: Click "Instagram Ads"

⚙ **General**

📭 Messaging

⚙ Edit Page

📧 Post Attribution

🔔 Notifications

💬 Messenger Platform

👤 Page Roles

👥 People and Other Pages

👥 Preferred Page Audience

🎁 Partner Apps and Services

◎ Instagram Ads

★ Featured

🖼 Instant Articles

🎥 Crossposting

💬 Page Support Inbox

ⓘ Place Tips

$ Payments

Step 2: Click "Add an Account"

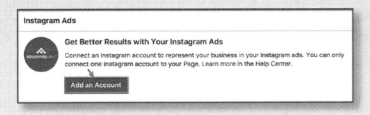

Instagram Ads

Get Better Results with Your Instagram Ads
Connect an Instagram account to represent your business in your Instagram ads. You can only connect one Instagram account to your Page. Learn more in the Help Center.

Add an Account

Step 3: Click "Add an existing account"

If you already have an existing, active Instagram account, choose the first option then enter your Instagram username and password. If you don't already have an existing Instagram account, choose the second option to create an account.

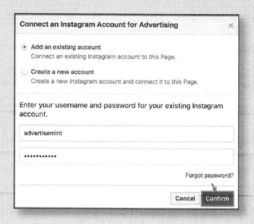

Step 4: You're done

Blocking Words and Profanity

Cyberbullies and trolls are a menace to the internet. Often they prowl the comments section, looking for an opportunity to insult, argue with, and annoy other internet users. I don't know about you, but I certainly don't want cyberbullies trolling my page and my followers. Fortunately, you have the ability to block certain words and profanity from being posted on your page. There are many reasons why you should filter offensive words and profanity, just in case you don't think doing so is worth the effort.

1. It maintains a safe place for people to share ideas.

2. It keeps your page clean and professional.

3. It encourages people to return to your page.

If you want all three, then I recommend filtering offensive words and profanity from your page.

How to Block Words

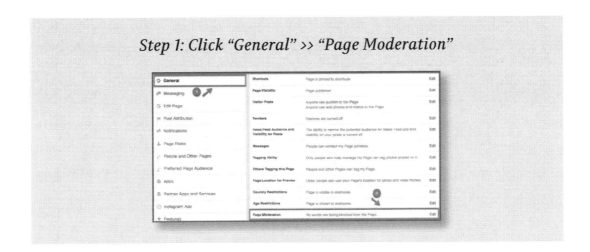

Step 1: Click "General" >> "Page Moderation"

Step 2: Enter words to block >> click "Save Changes"

Step 3: You're Done

Facebook will immediately mark the blocked words as spam as soon as they appear on your page.

How to Filter Profanity

Filtering profanity works differently than blocking words. While you choose the words you want to block, Facebook determines which profane language to block based on commonly reported words and phrases marked as offensive by the community. It also blocks profanity according to the degree you choose. Choosing medium will block moderately vulgar profanity while choosing strong will block only strongly vulgar profanity.

Step 1: Click "Profanity Filter" >> Choose degree >> save

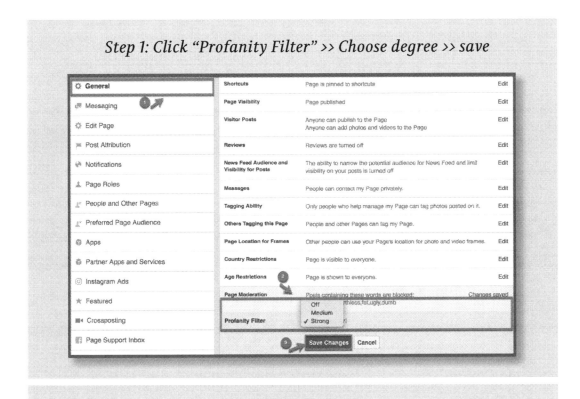

Step 2: You're done

Profanities that fall under the degree you chose will be blocked from appearing on your page.

Adding Features and Followers

Adding a profile picture and filling out your page information, which you did in chapter 3, is not enough. You need to make your page look thorough, professional, and active. In this section I discuss the four important things you must add to your Facebook page: verifications, followers, CTA buttons, and cover photos.

Verifying Your Facebook Page

If you own a Facebook page categorized under local business, company, or organization, then your page is eligible for a gray verification badge. You've likely seen this before. Have you ever noticed small blue check marks next to celebrities' profile photos on various social media networks such as Facebook, Instagram, or Twitter? Then you've seen a verification badge. Verification badges let your page visitors know that your page is authentic. While blue verification badges are for public figures, celebrities, and brands, gray verification badges are for businesses and companies.

If you want to verify your page, you can do so from your page's settings. Note, however, that only pages with a profile and cover photo are eligible. If you own a Facebook page categorized under local business, company, or organization but you don't have a profile or cover photo, then you're not eligible for the badge. You can verify your page in two ways: with a phone number or with a document. I'll show you how to do both.

Verifying Your Facebook Page with a Phone Number

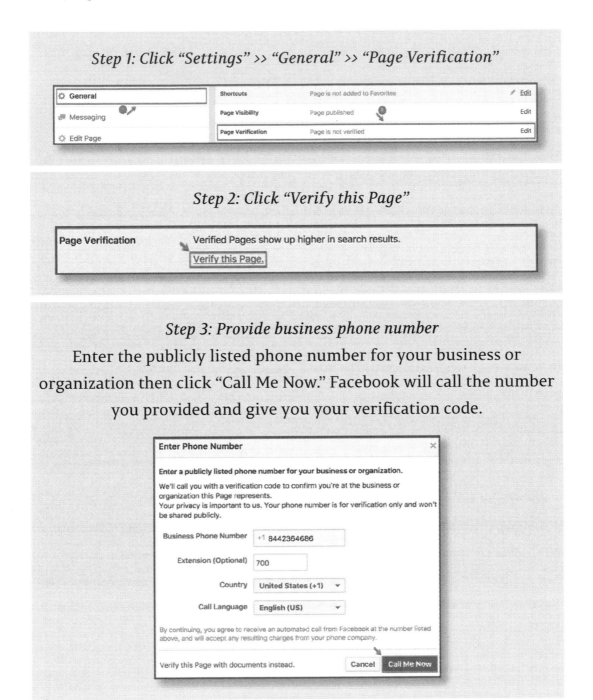

Step 1: Click "Settings" >> "General" >> "Page Verification"

Step 2: Click "Verify this Page"

Step 3: Provide business phone number

Enter the publicly listed phone number for your business or organization then click "Call Me Now." Facebook will call the number you provided and give you your verification code.

Step 4: Enter verification code

Verifying Your Page with a Document

Step 1: Click "Verify this Page with documents instead"

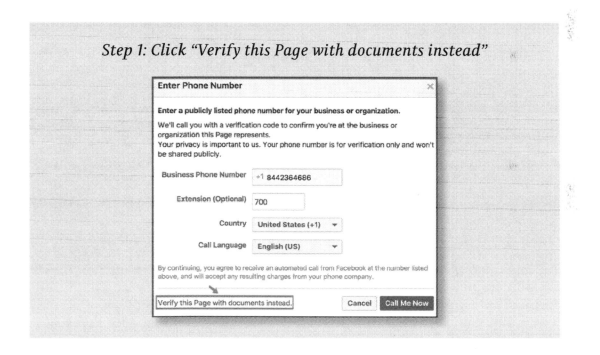

Step 2: Upload Document

You can upload a business utility or phone bill, business license, business tax file, certificate of formation, or articles of incorporation. The information you share will not be shared to the public.

Step 3: Wait

You will receive a confirmation stating that the document you provided is under review. You will hear from Facebook via email within a few days.

Uploading a Cover Photo to Your Page

This might sound silly, but I would never dare run a page that didn't have a cover photo. Not only is it required to obtain a verification badge (it's that important), but it also adds style, personality, and aesthetic appeal to your page. There's a reason it's hard to find a Facebook page with no cover photo (go on, try it. I challenge you). Without one, your page may look bare and unfinished.

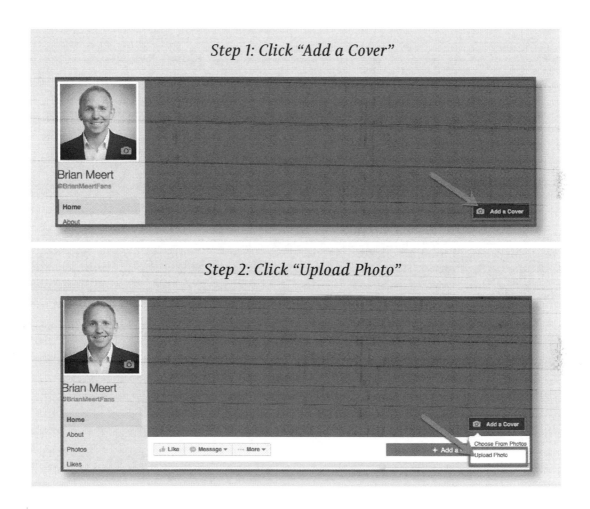

Step 1: Click "Add a Cover"

Step 2: Click "Upload Photo"

Step 3: Choose photo

Step 4: Drag to reposition photo and save

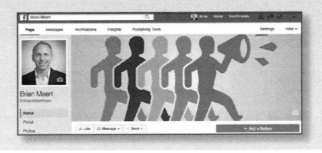

Step 5: You're done

Adding a CTA Button to Your Page

CTA buttons are a great way to encourage followers and page visitors to make a desired action. CTA buttons can encourage them to shop at your online store, book an appointment, learn more about your business, and sign up for email notifications, among numerous others. With CTA buttons, you can easily and quickly connect with a potential customer.

Step 1: Click "Add a Button"

Step 2: Add CTA button >> Website URL >> iOS destination

The website URL will direct users to the URL's landing page after they have clicked on the button.

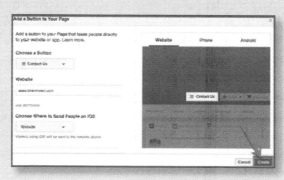

Step 3: Promote your button

Doing so will notify followers about your new button.

Step 4: You're done

Inviting Your Friends to Like Your Page

The purpose of starting a Facebook page is mute when you don't collect followers. How do you begin? How do you start a following? To start, you can invite Facebook friends to like your page.

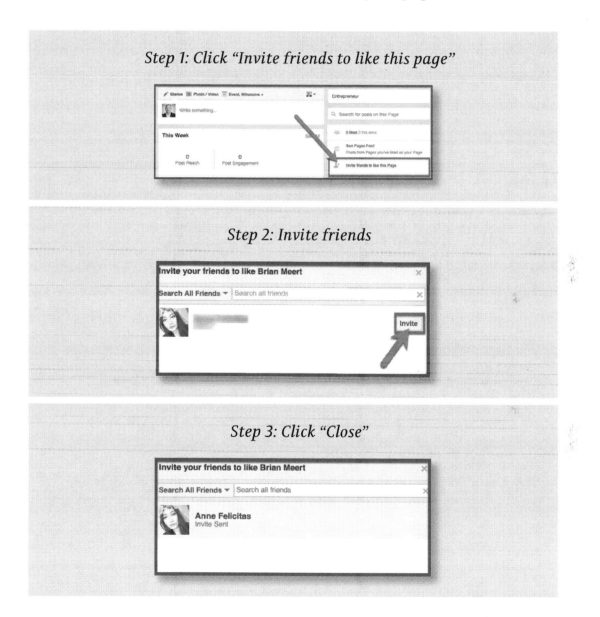

Step 1: Click "Invite friends to like this page"

Step 2: Invite friends

Step 3: Click "Close"

Important Page Tools

Creating a Facebook pages opens doors to your business. With a Facebook page, you can get data on your audience, easily connect with your followers, and create promotions—and that's only a few of the things you can do. However, before you can use your page to its full potential, you must know what the important page tools are and where you can find them. Fortunately, I've listed all of the important page tools in this section so you won't have to spend hours searching for them.

Messages

Keeping in contact with your followers allows you to appear more approachable and friendly. The more approachable and friendly you are, the more likely fans will remain loyal and the less likely they'll unfollow your page. You can more intimately connect with your fans with Messenger, which is accessible from the page header and from the menu options underneath your cover photo.

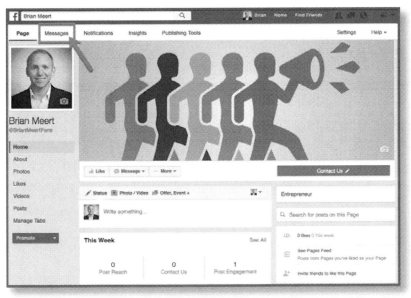

Figure 10.3

Figure 10.4

Notifications

You are likely familiar with the little globe-shaped button on the upper right side of Facebook that stores all of your notifications. This is different from the notifications tab located on your Facebook page. Although Facebook notifications show both notifications from your profile and your page, the notifications tab from your page only shows page notifications.

Notifications are important because they keep you updated on activity within your page. If someone comments, likes, reposts, or reacts to any of your posts, Facebook will notify you so you can respond and interact with your followers. When you interact with your followers, you encourage them to engage with your content and remain subscribed to your page.

Figure 10.5

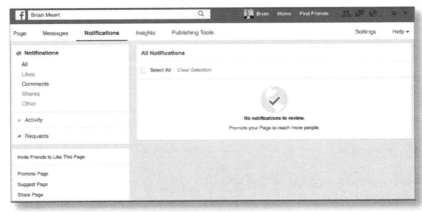

Figure 10.6

Insights

Insights, which keeps you updated on your pages' performance, lets you view your followers' activity on your page. For example, you can view the data on your page's views, likes, and reach. When you visit your insights page, you will see a list of subsections to the left.

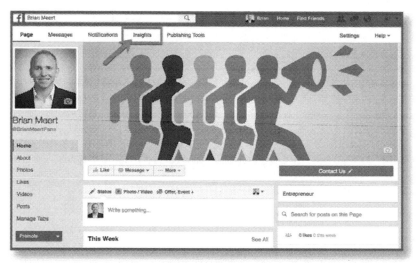

Figure 10.7

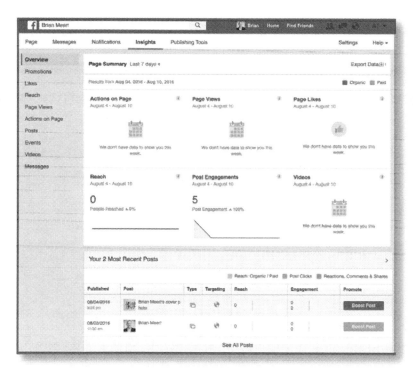

Figure 10.8

- **Overview:** Shows a summary of page activities from the last seven days. Information includes page views, page likes, reach, video views, and page followers.

- **Promotions:** Allows you to create and buy promotions for four types of page objectives: increasing calls, increasing website visitors, increasing local awareness, and promoting your page. Think of promotions as ads for your page.

- **Followers:** Provides data on the sources of your page follows and your total followers. The data for the latter can be broken down by unfollows, organic followers, paid followers, and net followers.

- **Likes:** Provides data on page likes. You can view a benchmark report that compares your average likes over time along with organic likes, paid likes, new likes, and unlikes. You can also view where your page likes occurred, whether it occurred on your ads, your page, or on mobile.

- **Reach:** Provides data on your posts' total reach and engagement.

- **Page views:** Provides data on total page views. You can view the age and gender of the individuals who viewed your page; their country and city; the device the view occurred on; and the source of the view.

- **Actions on page:** Provides data on the total actions on your page, including clicks to get directions, to call, and to go to a website.

- **Posts:** Provides data on your posts. You can view data on when your followers are online, which posts received the most engagement, and how much engagement each post received.

- **Events:** Provides data on your events. You can view data on reach, views, engagement, ticket sales, and audience.

- **Videos:** Provides performance insights on your videos. Information includes the minutes viewed and total video views.

- **People:** Provides insights on your followers. Information includes their age, gender, and country. You can also see which demographic engages more with your content.

- **Local:** Provides insights on people within your location. Information includes activity and peak hours, demographics of people near you, and people near you who were reached by your ads.

- **Messages:** Provides data on total conversations.

- **Instant Articles CTA:** Provides data on CTAs in Instant Articles. Information includes total sign-ups, total impressions, sign-ups by age and gender, and sign-ups by location.

Publishing Tools

Managing your business's social media is time consuming. Posting twice a day every day takes a lot of work and disrupts the normal flow of your schedule. Publishing tools is a godsend to those who struggle with managing social media. Publishing tools makes your job a lot easier by allowing you to schedule posts that will automatically publish on your selected date—it's a free social media automated tool. Instead of paying for a monthly fee, you can use publishing tools instead.

Scheduling Posts

Step 1: Click "Schedule"

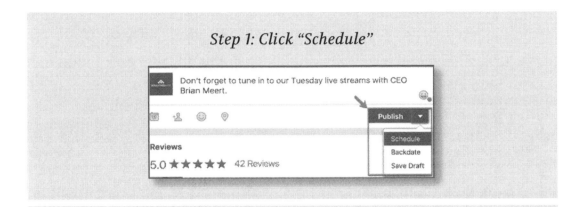

Step 2: Set date >> click "Schedule"

Step 3: You're done

Your scheduled posts will appear in your publishing tools under "Scheduled."

CHAPTER 11: FACEBOOK RESOURCES

Best Digital Advertising Blogs

As a Facebook advertiser, it's important that you keep yourself well informed of the latest trends and news in digital advertising. If Facebook added a new feature to Ads Manager, you would want to be the first to know. To keep myself informed, I often read articles and blogs from several websites, including Jon Loomer's, another Facebook ads expert; AdEspresso; and Business 2 Community. Here are the top ten sources I use to keep myself informed of the changes in the digital advertising world.

Facebook for Business[13]

Facebook for Business is a good source for people who want to know the latest Facebook advertising updates. It covers changes made to Business Manager; additions to social media features such as Messenger, news feed, and Facebook Live; and announcement on events such as the Annual Facebook Awards. Unlike most tech publications and digital advertising blogs, which derive their Facebook news from Facebook for Business, Facebook's business blog includes

---

13   https://www.facebook.com/business/

video tutorials that accompany their posts as well as Q&As for those with burning inquiries and success stories. If you want to know everything about Facebook's world, this is the website to visit.

Advertising Age[14]

Advertising Age, although also specializing in entertainment and world news, provides news related to digital advertising. It has covered news related to Super Bowl ads and Facebook's attempts to copy Snapchat, among numerous others. If you want to read opinion pieces and news about current digital advertising trends, then *Advertising Age* is a great resource to look at.

Mashable[15]

Much like *Advertising Age*, Mashable also covers news about the latest in technology, current events, business, and entertainment. Unlike *Advertising Age* and Facebook for Business, however, it doesn't cover news about Facebook advertising. Rather, it focuses on social media stories, such as the rivalry between Facebook and Snapchat, and social media features that have launched or that are being tested. If you're interested in social media updates, *Mashable* is the way to go.

Jon Loomer[16]

If you want more help with the nitty-gritty of Ads Manager and Power Editor, then you should read Jon Loomer's blog. Comprising product updates, how-to guides, podcasts, free webinars, strategies, and best practices, Loomer's blog is dedicated solely to Facebook advertising.

---

14   http://adage.com/

15   http://mashable.com/

16   https://www.jonloomer.com/

AdEspresso[17]

Have you ever asked yourself whether an ad with an emoji on the copy performs better than an ad without an emoji? Maybe you've wondered whether an ad image with a man outperforms an ad image with a woman. If you want access to guides and best practices that have been tested and proven, then AdEspresso is the resource for you. AdEspresso, a platform that allows you to easily manage your Facebook ads, provides information on A/B test results and digital advertising guides for Facebook, Instagram, YouTube, and Snapchat.

Business 2 Community[18]

A good resource for advertising best practices and tips, this website contains hundreds of guest posts from marketers, advertisers, entrepreneurs, and social media experts from around the globe. These guest writers share some of their tips and tricks, how-tos, guides, and best practices on their mastered industry. You'd find any topic related to marketing and advertising here.

eMarketer[19]

eMarketer, which grants you access to charts, articles, interviews, case studies, web conferences, and videos, among numerous others, is the best source for research and data on e-commerce, B2B content, search marketing, advertising budgets and spending, and social media.

---

17   https://adespresso.com/

18   http://www.business2community.com/

19   https://www.emarketer.com/

Social Media Examiner[20]

A source very similar to Business 2 Community, Social Media Examiner provides step-by-step how-to blogs, product updates, podcasts, and guides for the business, marketing, and advertising industries. Business 2 Community has content for Facebook, Instagram, and Twitter advertisers.

Nanigans[21]

Nanigans, a company that offers advertising software for in-house advertisers, is a treasure trove for all sorts of resources: digital advertising-related blogs, ebooks, case studies, reports, videos, tools, and infographics. Visit this site if you're looking for advertising tips and tricks, insights verified by research, and benchmark reports for various social media advertising platforms.

Instagram's Blog[22]

Although not the best resource for advertising, Instagram's blog, which focuses on human interest and celebrity stories, is the place to check for Instagram-related updates. If you're interested in the changes or additions made to its platform and policies, Instagram's blog is the best place to go.

---

20   http://www.socialmediaexaminer.com/

21   http://www.nanigans.com/blog/

22   http://blog.instagram.com/

Contact Links

You would be hard-pressed to find someone who enjoys searching for Facebook support. Contacting Facebook support often involves going from one web page to the other until you finally find the right contact form an hour later. The list I provide here contains links to contact forms for Facebook advertising and payment issues as well as to applications for developers and mobile carriers. Remember to log in to your Facebook account to gain access to these links. They will not appear to you otherwise. Once you've submitted your form, Facebook's support team will contact you within one business day.

Facebook and Instagram Advertising Issues
https://www.facebook.com/business/support/contact-us
Payment Issues
https://www.facebook.com/help/contact/1129731163763184
Credit Card Issues
https://www.facebook.com/help/contact/?id=139470636104003
Ads API Application
https://www.facebook.com/business/standardadsapi
Pending Facebook Ads Issues
https://www.facebook.com/help/contact/515460121837726/
Partners
I'm a mobile carrier who wants to partner with Facebook Home
https://www.facebook.com/help/contact/?id=555823267772403
I'm a mobile operator, and I want access to the Mobile Partner Program
https://www.facebook.com/help/contact/774119655987777

Figure 11.1 Links to Facebook's contact forms

Messenger Bots

I won't blame you if you haven't heard of Messenger bots before. Slightly new to Facebook, this helpful tool doesn't appear in tech publications and blogs as often as other features do like Stories, Facebook Live, and VR. In fact, these bots exist covertly: they don't appear to you unless you search for them or unless you message a business with a bot installed. Although a slightly extraneous topic, it didn't feel right to omit Messenger bots from this book. Granted, as a beginner, Messenger bots are the least of your worries. In fact, you will probably never use Messenger bots in your entire advertising career, but I can

Figure 11.2
A conversation with a chatbot

foresee this tool gaining popularity in the future, and I wanted you to know of this option in case it will help you manage your business. For those reasons, I'm dedicating this small section to Messenger bots: what they are, where you can learn more about them, and where you can create them.

Messenger bots, 100,000 of which currently exist on Messenger, are AI chatbots that send automated messages on behalf of businesses. When a customer sends a message to a business, the bot will recognize the keywords and the vocabulary of the message and respond accordingly with a selection of relevant actions, such as visiting a website, booking an appointment, making a purchase or, as someone from my team found during election season, registering to vote. If you want to interact with a chatbot, simply visit Messenger and enter the name of the business you want to contact. Once you click the bot you want to interact with from the search option, a conversation between you and the bot will open, including a greeting from the bot to start you off.

These are several companies that will create Messenger bots for you.

- ChatFuel
- Botsify
- Kik
- OnSequel
- It's Alive
- Rebotify
- ChattyPeople
- MEOKAY
- Smooch
- Beep Boop
- BotKit
- FlowXO

Figure 11.3 Companies that create Messenger bots

These are resources that provide helpful information and how-tos about chatbots.

- **Facebook for Developers:** tools, support, news, videos, and documents

- **Chatbot Academy:** how-to blogs and courses

- **Chatbot Magazine:** tutorial and news

- **Chatbot:** case studies and news

- **Botswiki:** tutorials and articles

Figure 11.4 Chatbot resources

CHAPTER 12: THE PSYCHOLOGY OF FACEBOOK ADS

The Five Ps of Marketing and Other Elements

There are several reasons people purchase, reasons that are often referred to in marketing books as the five *P*s. The five *P*s are product, price, placement, promotion, and people. If used correctly, the five *P*s can push your customers to convert.

Product

Customers will most likely purchase from you when you offer a superior product or service that meets their needs. Let's say a customer is considering buying two cars that are identical in size, color, and speed. However, one car gets twenty-five miles to the gallon and the other gets fifty miles to the gallon. If that customer has long commutes, she will most likely purchase the car with the better gas mileage. When it comes to Facebook ads, you need to show customers that your product or service is better than your competitors'.

Price

Customers will also most likely purchase from you when your product is fairly priced, especially in comparison to your competitors' prices. If your and your competitors' products are similar in appearance, type, and functionality, customers will most likely purchase the product with the lowest price (unless they delight in purchasing the most expensive products in an ostentatious display of wealth). It's important that you sell a product with a competitive price, especially during a time when customers can easily compare prices online.

Placement

Another element that compels customers to buy is placement, or the location of your product. Imagine coming across a man selling cold bottled water as you trek through a blisteringly hot desert. Incredibly thirsty, you ask to buy one, and the man says he charges six dollars, a ridiculous amount. You buy anyway because you're thirsty and desperate. The water man succeeds in ripping you off because he is at the location where the demand and need for his product is high. Similarly, strategic placement of your Facebook ad is key. For example, if you own multiple brick-and-mortar stores, you can create store location ads to target people within your store location, or you can place ads in areas that your audience frequently visits, whether that's on mobile news feed, desktop news feed, or right column.

Promotion

A promotion can quickly urge your customers to bite on your offer like a hungry bass biting on a fisher's hook. Promotions are more than just good deals—they're temporary deals that, due to the sense of urgency and exclusivity they instill, cause customers to hastily purchase. Imagine you're shopping for a new credit card. You find two cards with the same APR, same spending limit, and same bonus travel points. However, one card charges you zero percent interest on purchases for the first eighteen months. You would choose the zero percent APR credit card, of course, because it's a better deal. Offering a promotion can often be a strong tactic to drive customers to purchase your product rather than your competitors' products.

People

The fifth P, people, pertains to friends' and public figures' influence on someone's purchase decision. Experts believe that customers are more likely to purchase a product when it has been recommended or praised by friends, family, a public figure, or a celebrity. Recommendations and praises from these people are called social proof. Social proof is so effective, in fact, numerous companies scramble to work with influencers to gain it. That's why you often see ads feature a celebrity or why public figures sponsor brands.

Adding social proof is an important strategy. Although there are multiple ways you can include social proof, such as adding customer reviews to your ad creatives or partnering with influencers, all news feed ads contain social proof by default. Much like regular Facebook posts, news feed ads also have comments and engagement sections on the bottom of the ad that function as social proof by showing users how many engagements (likes, comments, reactions, and shares) the ad has received from the public.

Figure 12.1 An example of social proof

When creating your Facebook ads, always keep the five Ps in mind. Remember that the quality of the product, the price, the location of your ad, the promotion, and the recommendations and praises by others pare five elements that may push customers to purchase.

Evoking Emotions

If there's one thing that's true about humans, it's that they are impatient. You've seen it: a frustrated man honking at still cars in traffic, an exasperated woman tapping her feet impatiently as she waits in line at the DMV. You've undoubtedly felt untethered rage while waiting for your slow web browser to load. In a fast-moving world, we want things to move quickly. If people are naturally impatient in their day-to-day lives, you can imagine how impatient they are when browsing the Internet. On Facebook, especially, every second matters. People scan through their news feeds faster than ever. On average, a user will view your ad on a mobile news feed for 1.7 seconds and for 2.5 seconds on a desktop news feed.[23] You have around three seconds to grab users' attention with an ad that is relevant to them. There are a few ways you can do that. First, you can stop them mid scroll by creating eye-catching, high-quality creatives and compelling, concise copies. Then you maintain their attention by creating an ad that evokes emotions, spurring them to purchase. If you want to compel your audience, you have to manipulate their emotions, whether that's instilling a sense of urgency, kinship, or difficulty.

Urgency

Creating a sense of urgency is one of the best ways to compel a user to complete a desired action. In fact, some of the most successful ad campaigns I've ran are the ones that instill a sense of urgency, with copies that announce "24 hour sale" and "this deal expires at midnight." I've seen its effectiveness, and it is no surprise that this is a tactic popular among advertisers. There's one emotion that makes the urgency tactic effective: fear. People fear a lost opportunity, and people fear regret. When creating your ad, manipulate your customers' fears. Make them believe that they will regret ignoring your offer.

---

23   Facebook data, Q3 2015.

Scarcity

Much like urgency, by instilling a sense of scarcity, you play on people's fear of a lost opportunity. When people think a product is in low supply, they feel compelled to take action, fearing the loss of the item. Scarcity tactics often work well alongside sales or discounts that provide the benefit of buying your product. Examples of copies that instill a sense of urgency are "only 50 left at this price" and "first 25 people get this special offer." Although scarcity tactics can increase sales, it's wise not to overuse them because you would cause customers to become skeptical and, consequently, doubtful of your brand. For example, your customers may become skeptical when your deal-ends-in-24-hours ad continues to run for a week.

Difficulty

If there's one adage that has followed me from economics class in high school to present day, it's "there's no such thing as a free lunch." The adage communicates a valuable lesson all advertisers must learn: nothing comes for free. If you obtain a product for free, someone else must pay the price. For that reason, free giveaways may ring false to your customers. They may believe that a giveaway that is too good to be true is simply that—too good to be true. People's skepticism, their fear of unrealistic offers, is justified considering the number of scam ads that exist on the Internet, promising victims free items that cost double the original price of shipping, that will never arrive in their mailboxes, or that are of extremely low quality. For skeptical buyers wary of scams, the word "free" can often be equated with too good to be true.

To alleviate your customers' skepticism, you can offer free items as an incentive to take a certain action. Try offering free items once customers have liked or followed your page, taken your short survey, or left a positive review about your business. By using free items as incentives, you're giving skeptics a realistic offer that will help to allay their doubts.

Kinship

If you want customers to be more receptive to your ad, you must speak to them as if you were one of their own. After you position yourself as your customers' peer, they will be more likely to respond to your ad because people tend to accept those who are similar to them. To be more relatable to your customers, try speaking their language in your copy. That means speaking like a twenty-one-year-old woman if you have to (as I do with the ads for one of my clients who sells women's clothing) or speaking like a sixty-year-old man (as I also do for another client who sells gold IRAs). Once you connect your brand with your customers, your ad will be more effective.

The Psychological Impact of Colors

It's highly unlikely that you'll pay much attention to your ad's color scheme. In fact, you likely won't give the color scheme any thought at all. Black, brown, purple, or fuchsia—it makes no difference to you. On the contrary, color does make a difference. Color, as it turns out, evokes certain feelings and tones that can influence your audience's psychology.

Yellow	optimism, clarity, youthfulness, warmth, and cheerfulness
Orange	friendship, cheerfulness, confidence, warmth, intuition, optimism, spontaneity, cordiality, freedom, impulsiveness, motivation, excitement, enthusiasm, caution, aggression, action, courage, success
Red	excitement, youthfulness, boldness, passion, activity, energy, leadership, willpower, confidence, ambition, power, hunger, love, appetite, urgency
Purple	creativity, imagination, wisdom, eccentricity, originality, individualism, wealth, modesty, compassion, eminence, respect, fantasy, royalty, success
Dark blue	trust, trustworthiness, strength, order, loyalty, sincerity, authority, communication, confidence, peace, integrity, control, responsibility, success, tranquility, masculinity, water, serenity, satiation, coldness, productivity, security
Light blue	spirituality, thoughtfulness, contentedness, control, help, determination, self-sufficiency, modernity, goals, awareness, purpose, accessibility, ambition

Green	peacefulness, growth, health, balance, restoration, equilibrium, positivity, nature, generosity, clarity, prosperity, good judgement, safety, stability, health, tranquility, money, growth, relaxation, wealth, fertility
Gray	balance, neutrality, tranquility
Pink	love, tranquility, respect, warmth, femininity, intuition, care, assertiveness, sensitivity, nurture, possibilities
Brown	friendliness, the earth, the outdoors, longevity, conservatism
Tan/beige	dependability, flexibility
Turquoise	spirituality, healing, protection, sophistication
Silver	glamor, technology, gracefulness, sleekness
Gold	wealth, prosperity, value, tradition
Black	protection, drama, class, formality
White	goodness, innocence, purity, freshness, ease, cleanliness

Image 12.2 The different psychological impacts of colors

CHAPTER 13: CREATIVE BEST PRACTICES

Because your ad's design is important, it would be a crime to teach you how to create Facebook ads without teaching you how to create them well. Over the years, I've discovered the best ways to create Facebook ads. Some of the discoveries were the result of my own experience A/B testing different creatives for my clients and some come from my extensive readings about creative best practices. In this chapter, I give you tips on how to improve your copies, images, and videos.

Copy

When creating copies, you must know your audience. Know who you're writing for, know how that person thinks, and know what that person needs. To know your audience, create a fictional character, a persona, who possesses the same demographics, behaviors, attitudes, lifestyles, and needs as your target audience. Let's say you're selling designer handbags. Which group is likely to purchase your products? Affluent women ages twenty-five to fifty would most likely buy those products. Why would they want those products? They want to stay in fashion, they want to stay relevant, or they want to flaunt their wealth. After you've created your persona, use it to craft your copies. When you speak to your audience, speak to them as if you were a woman aged twenty-five to fifty who wanted to stay in fashion, relevant, or flaunt her wealth. Only then will your audience be able to relate to you and to trust you enough to buy your product.

Next, your copy must not sound too salesy. Remember that your audience is on social media to socialize with peers rather than to buy your products. Because your audience has zero buying intent, they are more likely to feel annoyed by ads. So your ads must take a gentle selling approach. Rather than pushing a sale, suggest an idea and provide a solution to a problem that shows your audience what life would be like with the product. For example, instead of scrawling a giant "BUY THIS GREAT PRODUCT NOW" copy across your ad, try something like this: "Finally, you can get rid of those pesky, persistent stains." Unlike the first copy, the second copy provides a solution to a problem and a reason for your audience to buy without pushing hard on the sale.

Finally, you must know how to leverage headline formats that have historically worked for you. Here are some popular templates you can test:

- How to
  How to remove carpet stains in 3 seconds

- Listicle
  Five ways to quickly remove carpet stains

- Who else wants [your product or benefits of the product]?
  Who else wants an easy way to get rid of carpet stains?

- The secret of [beneficial insider knowledge]
  The secret of removing carpet stains in 3 seconds

- Here is a method that is helping [your target audience] to [a helpful benefit]
  Here is a method that is helping moms quickly and easily remove carpet stains

- Little known ways to [a solution to a problem or a benefit]
  Here are little known ways to remove carpet stains in 3 seconds

- Get rid of [a problem] once and for all
  Get rid of those pesky carpet stains once and for all

- Here's a quick way to [solve a problem]
  Here's a quick way to remove carpet stains

- Now you can [have something desirable] [great circumstances]
  Now you can quit your job and make even more money

- [Do something] like [world-class example]
  Remove carpet stains like Mr. Clean

- Have a [blank] you can be proud of
  Have a clean carpet you can be proud of

- Build a [blank] you can be proud of
  Build a career you can be proud of

- What everybody needs to know about [blank]
  What everybody needs to know about removing carpet stains

Images

Your ad's image is the most important, most dominant part of your ad because, due to its large size, it's the first thing users see. Unfortunately, your image only has a few seconds to capture the attention of users rapidly scrolling through their feeds. To stop them mid scroll, use images with eye-catching colors that are vibrant and that contrast against elements within the ad or against the news feed. When choosing an image for your ad, never choose an image with a light background because it would blend in with the feed. If you're using stock photos, do use color overlays to place over your stock photos—a great way to make stock photos less recognizable and more unique to you. After all, because stock photos are open for use by everyone, it's very likely that other advertisers are using those photos too.

You can also improve your photos by adding text on the image. If you want to quickly communicate your point to busy, impatient Facebook users, add your CTA or offer on the image itself. This will allow you to communicate your message as quickly as possible on the area of your ad that receives the most attention. When adding text to your images, you must remember to abide by Facebook's 20 percent rule, a rule that has confounded me, my team, and numerous other Facebook advertisers. The rule states that texts in ads cannot be more than 20 percent of the image. (See the chapter on Facebook's ad policies for more details.) If you don't want to break this rule and risk the approval of your ads, then make sure that your text does not dominate the image.

People and Objects

Slapping a few words on a colored background, dusting your hands off in self-satisfaction, and calling it a day is not the best way to create your ad images. You have to try different types of images, such as images featuring people or objects. In fact, some research shows that images with relatable and recognizable people perform better than images without recognizable people. Research conducted by Keywee, a company that helps publishers successfully advertise their content, revealed that ad images with recognizable people outperformed ads with unrecognizable people.[24] That's because people trust those they recognize. This tactic is so popular that many brands scramble to hire celebrities who can sponsor their products: Kylie Jenner for Sugar Bear Hair, John Malkovich for Squarespace, and Selena Gomez for Coke, to name a few. These well-known celebrities lend brands more credibility, and they can even sway their fans into buying the products they're promoting.

You can also add credibility to your ad by featuring the logos, objects, and symbols of widely recognized companies. Of course, I'm not saying that you should steal other brands' logos and symbols. Rather, include them in your ad if your product or service integrates with those brands. For example, if you're an advertiser promoting your advertising agency's services and you work with big brands such as Victoria's Secret, Coke, and Nike, include those logos in your image. Associating those big brands that people know, use, and trust with yours will give your business credibility.

---

24 "All Things Creative: Creating Facebook Posts that Convert—Keywee." Keywee, January 31, 2017, accessed July 26, 2017, http://keywee.co/all-things-creative-building-facebook-ads-that-convert/.

If you choose to feature objects rather than people in your Facebook ads, go a step further and feature your products. Doing so will achieve two things. First, if the featured product looks attractive in the image, people will be more likely to click on the ad. Second, if you feature your product in the ad, people will be able to imagine themselves with your product. They will be able to see the product in their hands, see what their life will be with it. You can help your customers visualize your product in their lives by featuring a model or an actor using your product.

If you want to feature your own products in your ad, to show customers how they work and how they can be used, then I recommend using the carousel or video format. With a carousel ad, you can show the several ways customers can use your products in a string of carousel cards. Think of it as a how-to ad. Display each step in each carousel card with helpful images and instructional headlines to match. Do remember that you can only upload up to ten images in a carousel ad. The video format also works exceptionally well with how-to ads. I've done a few of those for several of my clients, and the results for those video ads are better than the results of the ads with static creatives. Because users prefer watching short videos, I always keep my video ads under one minute.

Video

If you're planning to use only single image ads for the rest of your advertising career, then forget it. Pack your bags, go home, and make a career change. Years of Facebook advertising drilled into my brain one important lesson: you must always try different ad formats to combat ad fatigue; users will overlook or ignore your ad if they have seen it too many times. An overused ad on news feed is like the guy telling the same joke at parties. People that hate to hear his overused joke avoid him at all costs. It's the same with ads. Tired of seeing the same ad on their feeds, users will quickly scroll past your ad, barely taking notice. Ad fatigue is your enemy. It will cause your relevancy scores to plummet and your costs to rise. To avoid ad fatigue, change your ad format—graduate from image ads to video ads.

Video, unlike the other ad formats, works exceptionally well with storytelling. With this type of moving creative, users can watch your story unfold, whether that story is about your product, your service, or your brand. My team and I often use video ads for a few of our clients, including one who sells magnetic mounts for electronic devices. We constantly create new videos for that client, videos in which actors use the mounts in their everyday lives. Video ads work well for us because the video allows us to tell a story about our client's product: how customers can use the product and how it can impact their lives.

There are four things you need to do when creating video ads. First, you have to make sure it's short, with a length of one minute at the most. Users will not likely watch the entirety of your video if it's too long. Second, place the story's important message within the first few seconds of the ad. Because viewers scroll out of a video if it has not captured their attention within the first fifteen seconds, it's crucial that you hook your viewers and communicate your message within those few precious seconds. Treat your videos like a news article following the pyramid format: use the most important points first followed by the least important points. While doing so, make sure that your video still makes logical sense according to your story. It should still be cohesive despite the inversion. Third, you should always create your videos for sound off because most users watch without sound. You can cater to those users by adding subtitles or including captions that encourage your viewers to watch with sound on. Fourth, make sure that your video's story is easily comprehensible even without captions or sound.

Incorporate the Three Es

When crafting your creatives, whether that's a photo, gif, or video, always remember to entertain, educate, and engage, which we marketers call the three *E*s. The three *E*s are so important to your ad's performance that you should ask your graphic designers to write them on a Post-it note and stick it on their computers.

Entertain

Social media users don't go to Facebook to shop. Rather, they go to Facebook to be entertained, whether that's by a meme, a video, or a friendly banter in the comments section. To catch people's attention, your ads should fulfill their need to be entertained. Make sure your ads make people smile, laugh, or cry. Make them experience love, wonder, mystery, or fear. Making sure your ads entertain your target audience is one way to improve your results.

Educate

Teaching people something they didn't know, such as a new skill or a little-known fact, is the second tactic to improving your results. Educational content will often cause curious and knowledge-hungry users to stop mid scroll. If you want to watch a few examples of great educational videos, watch the videos of Tasty, Tastemade, and Nifty, companies that successfully create helpful DIY videos that last less than two minutes. Media companies that create educational ads that provide solutions to problems work so well because they give users something in return for their time and attention: knowledge and a solution. For that reason, you should create content that educates your audience about your products and shows them how your products or services are the best solutions to their problems.

Engage

This is probably the most important of the three because Facebook's algorithm makes engagement essential to ads' and posts' rank on the feed. Posts that have a lot of engagement will appear higher on the feed than posts that have little engagement. This means you need to create irresistible ads that your target audience can't help but engage with. Sometimes engagement will happen effortlessly when you create killer ads that entertain or educate well. Sometimes, however, your ads will not have any engagement at all. If that's the case for you, then you need to encourage your audience to engage with your ad. For example, ask users for their opinions or feedbacks, or you can make a controversial statement that provokes a discussion. With every ad, you need to stop and ask yourself, "Am I talking to someone, or am I talking at someone?" You must speak to your audience in a way that will make them feel part of a conversation that they can easily participate in.

AFTERWORD

Congratulations, you made it. I commend your determination and patience by sticking through my how-tos and explanations until the end. If you feel like you don't need me anymore, that you can manage Facebook ads on your own, great. I'm happy that this book has helped you. Although you may feel like you know enough to be a Facebook advertising expert, I urge you to never stop asking questions, to never stop learning. Facebook advertising changes frequently. Nearly each month, Facebook announces a new feature or an update. The Business Manager you know now may change in a few months. For that reason, you must be eager to learn.

If after reading this book, you still have burning questions that need answering, or if upon dabbling with Facebook ads, you find yourself stumped, don't hesitate to use the resources I provided in this book or to connect with me. There are a few ways we can get in touch:

1. Connect through Social Media

You can reach me through email, Facebook, Instagram, Snapchat, and LinkedIn.

Email: feedback@advertisemint.com
Facebook: https://www.facebook.com/advertisemint
Instagram: https://www.instagram.com/advertisemint
Snapchat: https://www.snapchat.com/advertisemint
LinkedIn: https://www.linkedin.com/in/brianmeert

2. Join Our MasterMind Group

You can join our MasterMind group, a group of Facebook advertisers who will answer any of your inquiries. The group provides exclusive walkthroughs, live training, interviews, tips from the pros, and more.

3. Let's Talk on Clarity

If you want one-on-one time with me to help you solve your problems, you can find me on Clarity, a consulting website (www.clarity.fm/brianmeert).

Before we part ways, I want to leave you with three pieces of advice. First, keep your A/B tests simple. Test two things at a time. Don't overwhelm yourself. Second, check your account every day. Facebook ads are like newborns. They require a lot of time and attention to survive. If you don't constantly watch your accounts, you won't be able to prevent the ROIs of accounts from plummeting. Third, don't be afraid to make mistakes. When I started advertising on Facebook, a time when such a thing was still new, there were no instructional books to help me navigate through the platform. Completely alone in my endeavors, I had to master Facebook ads through trial and error. Don't penalize yourself too much when you make mistakes. Rather, learn from them and fix them the best way you can.

I hope this book has demystified the complexities of Facebook advertising, and I hope you pursue your endeavors as a Facebook advertiser. It is truly a revolutionary platform, and I wish you the best of luck on your campaigns. Now go forth and create Facebook ads.

GLOSSARY

A

A/B Testing

Also called split testing, this is a method in which advertisers test which ad elements, such as headlines, copy, images, calls to action, and targeting, work best on your target audience. A/B testing can help you compare the performance of multiple variables in a campaign and determine which one is best for your objectives.

Account Currency

The currency (i.e., dollar, peso, or euro) that is used by an ad account. Any charges will appear in the selected currency.

Account ID

A unique ID for an ad account represented by a series of unique numbers. It may be needed if you are sharing access with your account or determining the difference between two accounts with the same name. You can find your ad account number in the drop-down menu located on the top left corner of Ads Manager.

Account Settings

An area of Facebook where you can view and edit account preferences. For example, you can edit your name and email address, notification preferences, and security features.

Account Spending Limit

The budget you set for your entire ad account. Your spending limit, which you can adjust at any time, is optional.

Actions

The data type that shows all actions taken by users within twenty-four hours after viewing an ad or sponsored story in a campaign. You will only see this data if you are promoting a page, event, or app. Actions include page and post likes, event RSVPs, and app installs.

Activity Log

The activity log, which only you can see, contains all the posts you posted or people posted on your timeline. Activity logs for pages are only accessible to those who manage the page.

Ad Account

The grouping of all your specific ad activity. Your ad account includes different campaigns, ad sets, ads, and billing information. You can manage multiple ad accounts through Business Manager.

Ad Auction

The method advertisers use to purchase ads. In the auction process, all Facebook ads compete against one another, and the ad with the best bid and value score wins.

Ad ID

This unique numerical ID differentiates between every ad created. This number is normally provided to Facebook's support team when asking for support for a problem.

Ad Reports

Ad reports contain all of the important metrics pertaining to your ad. Reports, which can be scheduled and saved for future use, can include date ranges, graphs, customized columns, and tables. Ad reports can be created or exported to ad accounts in Ads Manager.

Ad Set

All targeting for Facebook ads is done on the ad set level. An ad set can include multiple ads, bidding preferences, a budget, and a schedule. You can create an ad set for each of your audience segments by making the ads within the ad set target the same audience. This will help you control the amount you spend on each audience, decide when each audience will see your ads, and see metrics specific to each audience.

Ad Set Budget

The budget you set when you create an ad set. Two types of budgets exist: the daily budget and the lifetime budget. The daily budget is the maximum amount you are willing to spend each day, whereas the lifetime budget is the amount you are willing to spend for the duration of your campaign.

Ad Targeting

Ad targeting contains all of the target options you choose to define for your target audience (e.g., location, gender, age, likes, interests, relationship status, workplace, and education). All Facebook ads require you to create a target audience using its over 850 targeting options.

Add to Cart

The number of times an item was added to a shopping cart on your website because of your ad.

Add to Cart Conversion Value

The total value that represents the number of items that were added to a cart on your website because of your ad.

Admin

Admins are people who manage the activity of ad accounts, fan pages, or Facebook groups. Admins also have the ability to post, moderate, or control content and to add or remove other users from account roles.

Ads API

The Ads API allows you to create and manage ads on Facebook programmatically. The API also allows Facebook Preferred Marketing Partners to build solutions for marketing automation with Facebook's advertising platform.

Ads Manager

The part of Business Manager where you can create ads and view, edit, and access performance reports for all of your campaigns, ad sets, and ads. You can also view all of your Facebook ad campaigns and payment history, change your bids and budgets, export ad performance reports, and pause or restart your ads at any time.

Advertising Policies

Facebook's advertising policies outlines the dos and don'ts of Facebook advertising, listing the types of ads that are restricted or forbidden. Violation of Facebook's policies will result in blocked accounts or rejected ads.

Amount Spent

The total amount you have spent during the dates you have selected in Ads Manager.

App Install Ads

Facebook ads that urge users to install an ad. Once clicked, the ad will direct users to the App Store or to Google Play to install the app.

App Installs

The number of times users have installed your app because of your ad.

App Uses

The number of times users have used your app because of your ad.

Audience

The group of people who can potentially see your ads.

Audience Insights

A Facebook tool designed to help marketers learn more about their target audience, including information about geography, demographics, lifestyle, and purchase behavior. With audience insights, advertisers can run reports on any Facebook user, including people connected to their fan page or people in a custom audience.

Audience Network

The Audience Network is a placement type that allows advertisers to place their ads in the apps and websites of Facebook's partners.

Audience Retention

A metric that measures the amount of time viewers are watching a video.

Augmented Reality (AR)

A technology that layers a digital image over a user's view of a physical, real-world environment. Unlike virtual reality (VR), which creates a digital 3-D simulation of the real world, augmented reality augments the environment with graphic overlays and special effects.

Autobid

Also known as Optimized CPM, autobid is a setting that automatically optimizes bids to reach an advertising goal by adjusting spend to reach users who are most likely to complete a goal, whether that goal is impressions, clicks, app installs, or conversions.

Average Cost Per Click (Average CPC)
The average cost per click for an ad.

Average Cost per Impression (Average CPM)
The cost incurred for every 1,000 impressions of an ad or for every 1,000 times an ad was displayed in front of a user.

Average Duration of Video Viewed
The average length of time people spent viewing a video. The average duration number is calculated by dividing the total video watch time by the play time.

Average Percent of Video Viewed
The average percentage of a video that people viewed. This number is calculated by dividing the total video view percentage by the total play time percentage.

B

Backup Payment Method
Additional optional payment methods that can be added to an ad account. If there is a problem with the primary payment method, Facebook will charge fees using the chosen backup payment method.

Bid
The amount advertisers pay to have an ad displayed on Facebook's platform.

Billing Summary

The billing summary lists all of advertisers' past and current ad charges. Each summary will contain a description link that, when clicked, will reveal to advertisers a detailed breakdown for the charge, including the dates that the charge covers and the specific ads that ran during that period.

Billing Threshold

A billing method that bills an account after an advertiser has spent a certain amount. Billing thresholds vary by country, and they comply with the currency and the payment method of an ad account. Billing thresholds determine when and how often advertisers are billed for their ads.

Blocking

The action that allows Facebook users to block someone from communication. Once blocked, a user cannot search for or view the Facebook profile of another user, cannot add that user as a friend, and cannot send or receive messages from that user.

Boosted Post

A boosted post is a regular post that you pay Facebook to advertise. Boosted posts, like Facebook ads, will appear on the news feeds of a target audience.

Broad Categories

The predefined targeting categories Facebook provides that groups users according to their likes and interests, the apps they use, and the pages they like, among other criteria.

Budget

The maximum amount you are willing to spend on each campaign.

Business Manager

A website that helps businesses and agencies manage their Facebook pages, ad accounts, and apps in one place. Business Manager also allows advertisers to centrally manage different permission levels of team members working on ad accounts or pages.

C

Call-to-Action Button (CTA Button)

The button that appears on a Facebook ad that takes users directly to a landing page. The button includes calls to action such as "shop now," "book now," "learn more," "sign up," "download," "shop more," "contact us," "apply now," and "donate now."

Campaign ID

A unique numerical ID associated with a campaign.

Campaign Level

The campaign level contains one or more ad sets and ads. When creating an ad at the campaign level, advertisers can choose an objective.

Campaign Spending Limit

A campaign spending limit allows advertisers to set an overall spending limit for an entire campaign. The limit stops all running ads once an account reaches the spending limit.

Canvas Ad

Canvas is an immersive Facebook ad that, once clicked, opens full screen in users' phones. Canvas ads can comprise videos, images, carousels, and call-to-action buttons, which users can swipe through, tilt for a panoramic view, or zoom in and out of.

Carousel Ad

Ads that include up to ten images or videos within a single ad unit that direct users to specific locations on a website. Each carousel ad contains up to ten carousel cards that users can swipe through and click.

Check-Ins

Check-Ins is a Facebook feature that allows users to tag a business location in their posts. Only businesses that have a Facebook business page with an address entered in the page's profile can appear as options for check-ins.

Checkouts

The number of times a checkout was completed on a website because of an ad.

Checkouts Conversion Value

The total value returned from conversions on a website because of an ad. Advertisers must have custom conversions enabled for this value to appear in their reports.

Clicks

Clicks is a metric that is measured by the number of times a user clicks on an ad. Clicks to like, share, or comment, as well as clicks on the CTA button, are measured as clicks.

Clicks to Play

Clicks to play is a metric that is measured by the number of times a video starts and plays for a minimum of three seconds after a person has clicked it. This metric is available for videos uploaded and embedded directly to Facebook. It is not, however, available for links to videos that play off Facebook.

Clicks to Play Video

The number of clicks to play a video because of your ad. This will include all video views regardless of whether the video played for more than three seconds.

Click-through Rate (CTR)

The number of clicks your ad receives divided by the number of times your ad is shown on the site (impressions) in the same time period. CTR All means the click-through rate for the total number of clicks you received—off-site clicks, likes, event responses—divided by the number of impressions.

Connections

Connections targeting is a targeting option in which advertisers can target or exclude the people who liked their page or location, installed their app, joined their event, used their app in the past thirty days, or checked in to their advertised location within twenty-four hours of viewing or clicking an ad or sponsored story.

Conversions

Conversions are the number of times people completed a desired action, such as purchases on a website or sign-ups for a newsletter.

Core Audiences

Core audiences is a targeting option that allows advertisers to reach precise audiences based on four main targeting types: location, demographic, interests, and behaviors. Facebook pulls data from the information users share on their profiles and the behaviors they exhibit online and offline.

Cost Per Action

The average amount advertisers pay for each action users make on their ads. Payment costs depend on the number of advertisers competing to show their ads to their target audience. Well-designed ads will encourage more people to take action, and the more actions garnered for the budget, the lower the cost per actions will be.

Cost Per All Actions

The average cost of all actions tracked by the Facebook pixel on a website after users viewed or clicked on an ad.

Cost Per App Engagement

The average cost per action on an app because of an ad.

Cost Per App Story Engagement

The average cost per action related to an app story because of an ad.

Cost Per App Use

The average cost for each app use because of an ad.

Cost Per Check-In

The average cost for each check-in because of an ad.

Cost Per Checkout (Conversion)

The average cost for each checkout on a website because of an ad.

Cost Per Click (CPC)

The amount advertisers pay each time a user clicks on their ads. The CPC for any ad is determined by the advertiser, and some advertisers may be willing to pay more per click than others. If advertisers bid on a CPC basis, they will be charged when users click on their ads and visit their websites. Total charges are based on the amount spent on the ad divided by all the clicks the ad received.

Cost Per Clicks to Play Video

The cost calculated by the number of times users viewed 50 percent of your video, including views that skipped to that point.

Cost Per Credit Spend Action

The average cost for each credit spend action because of an ad.

Cost Per Event Response

The average cost for each user who joins an event because of an ad.

Cost Per Gift Sale

The average cost of each gift sold on Facebook because of an ad.

Cost Per Key Web Page View (Conversion)

The average cost for each view of a key page on a website because of an ad.

Cost Per Lead (Conversion)

The average cost for each lead because of an ad.

Cost Per Mobile App Achievement

The average cost for each level-achieved action in a gaming app because of an ad.

Cost Per Mobile App Action

The average cost per action on an app because of an ad.

Cost Per Mobile App (Add to Cart)

The average cost for each add-to-cart action in a mobile app because of an ad.

Cost Per Mobile App (Add to Wish List)

The average cost for each add-to-wishlist action in a mobile app because of an ad.

Cost Per Mobile App Checkout

The average cost for each checkout in an app because of an ad.

Cost Per Mobile App Credit Spend

The average cost for each credit spend in an app because of an ad.

Cost Per Mobile App Feature Unlock

The average cost for each feature or achievement unlocked in an app because of an ad.

Cost Per Mobile App Install

The average cost for each app install because of an ad.

Cost Per Mobile App Payment Detail

The average cost for each added payment information on an app because of an ad.

Cost Per Mobile App Purchase

The average cost for each app purchase because of an ad.

Cost Per Mobile App Rating

The average cost for each rating of an app because of an ad.

Cost Per Mobile App Registration

The average cost for each registration in an app because of an ad.

Cost Per Mobile App Search

The average cost for each search in an app because of an ad.

Cost Per Mobile App Start

The average cost for each time a user starts an app because of an ad.

Cost Per Mobile App (Tutorial Completion)

The average cost for each tutorial completed on an app because of your ad.

Cost Per Offer Claim

The average cost for each offer claim because of your ad.

Cost Per 1,000 People Reached

The average cost advertisers pay to show their ads to 1,000 unique users.

Cost Per Other Mobile App Action

The average cost for other actions on an app because of an ad.

Cost Per Other Website Conversion

The average cost for each time a user took another action on a website because of your ad.

Cost Per Page Engagement

The average cost per engagement because of an ad.

Cost Per Page Like

The average cost per page like because of an ad.

Cost Per Page Mention

The average cost for each page mention as a result of an ad.

Cost Per Page Tab View

The average cost per tab views on a page as a result of an ad.

Cost Per Photo View

The average cost for each photo view as a result of an ad.

Cost Per Post Comment

The average cost for each comment on your page's posts as a result of your ad.

Cost Per Post Engagement

The average cost per engagement on a page's post as a result of your ad. This cost is calculated by dividing total spend by the total number of engagements.

Cost Per Post Like

The average cost for each like on your page's post as a result of an ad.

Cost Per Post Share

The average cost for each share on a page's post as a result of an ad.

Cost Per Question

The average cost for each question follow up as a result of an ad.

Cost Per Registration (Conversion)

The average cost for each registration on a website as a result of an ad.

Cost Per Ten-Second Video View

The average cost per ten-second video view, calculated as the amount spent divided by the number of ten-second video views.

Cost Per Thousand (CPM)

The average cost an advertiser pays for 1,000 impressions on an ad. If advertisers bid by CPM, they will be charged when users view their ads, regardless of whether they click on them.

Cost Per Unique Click (All)

The cost for the number of clicks an ad receives. Cost per unique clicks is calculated by dividing the number of clicks an ad receives by the number of impressions.

Cost Per Video View

The average cost per video view, which is calculated by dividing the amount spent by the number of video views.

Cost Per Website Action (All)

The average cost per website action tracked by the Facebook pixel on a website after users viewed or clicked on an ad.

Cover Photo

The cover photo is the large picture at the top of a Facebook profile, right behind the profile picture. All cover photos are public: anyone visiting a profile will be able to see it.

CPC (Link)

Cost per click to link is the amount charged each time someone clicks on a link in an ad that directs users off Facebook. Total charges are calculated by dividing the amount spent on the ad by the clicks to link.

Credit Spends

The number of times advertising coupons were spent in your app as a result of your ad.

Current Balance

The total amount spent on ads that haven't been billed yet. This balance will clear automatically after Facebook charges the account. The summary of charges can be found in the billing section under Ads Manager.

Custom Audience

A Custom Audience is an ad targeting option that allows advertisers to target an audience from an uploaded customer list. The list can comprise people from a customer file or people tracked by the Facebook pixel who have visited or took actions on a website, app, or Facebook page.

Custom Conversions

Custom conversions allow advertisers to track and optimize for conversions without adding anything to the Facebook pixel code placed in a site. Custom conversions can be used with Standard Events or URL-based variables. Custom conversions replaced the Facebook conversion pixel, which was discontinued in 2016.

D

Daily Active Users

This is the number of people who have viewed or interacted with a Facebook page on a specific day, categorized by the type of action they perform.

Daily Budget

The amount you've indicated you're willing to spend on a specific campaign per day. Facebook will never charge you more than your daily budget on a given day. Each ad set will have a separate budget. Ads will automatically stop showing once a daily budget for the ad set has been met for that day.

Daily Page Activity

This data breaks down the different ways people engage with a Facebook page on a specific day. (Engagement does not include comments and likes on posts.) The daily page activity will show when followers post, upload photos or videos on a business page (if enabled), write reviews, or mention the page in posts posted on their walls or on their friends' walls.

Daily Spend Limit

The daily spend limit is the maximum amount Facebook allows advertisers to spend in one day.

Delivery

The delivery status indicates whether a campaign, ad set, or ad is currently running.

Delivery Fatigue

A phenomenon in which an ad's performance may decline after it has been running for extended periods of time.

Desktop App Credit Spends Conversion Value

The total value returned from advertising coupons spent in a desktop app as a result of an ad. This is based on the value assigned to the conversion type in the pixel code.

Destination

The ad's destination is the landing page that users will land on after they click on an ad.

Device

The device on which the conversion event you're tracking occurred. For example, if someone converted on a desktop computer, the device on analytics will appear as desktop.

Dynamic Product Ads

Help businesses sell products online by showing relevant products from their catalog to the people who want to buy them. Dynamic product ads give marketers a powerful set of tools to promote the right product to the right person at the right time, and with a personalized message.

E

End Date

The date a campaign is scheduled to stop. Campaigns can run continuously or until specific dates.

Event Responses

The number of RSVPs for an event as a result of an ad.

External Referrers

The number of views a Facebook page received from website URLs that aren't part of Facebook.

F

Facebook Account Kit

The account kit helps users sign in to an app with their phone number or email address without the need for a password.

Facebook Analytics for Apps

Facebook Analytics for Apps provides analytics on developers' apps. The data includes information on audience insights such as age, gender, education, interests, country, language, and many more.

Aquila Drone

Aquila is Facebook's first full-scale drone for Internet.org. Using a linked network of the drones, Facebook plans to use Aquila to provide Internet access in remote parts of the world.

Project ARIES

Project ARIES (Antenna Radio Integration for Efficiency in Spectrum) is a terrestrial system focused on improving the speed, efficiency, and quality of Internet connectivity around the world. It provides a consistent, high-bandwidth Internet experience to both developing and developed economies that can suffer from insufficient data rates.

Facebook Audience Selector

The audience selector, a feature available to pages, allows page admins to select an audience for the content posted on the page.

Facebook Badge

A Facebook badge allows website owners to share their Facebook profiles, photos, or pages on their websites.

Facebook Event

Facebook event is a feature that lets users organize gatherings and respond to invites. Users can post statuses, upload photos, set dates, and enter event details to an event page.

Facebook Exchange (FBX)

The Facebook Exchange helps advertisers reach users who will potentially be interested in their offer. Interest is determined by the expressed interest in a similar type of offer online. This feature is typically used by advertisers who have data on users' intent to buy a product.

Facebook Friends

Facebook friends are people who are in a user's friends list on Facebook.

Facebook Lite

A version of Facebook that accommodates areas with low Internet connectivity by using less data.

Facebook Live API

Facebook Live API allows device manufacturers to integrate Facebook Live directly into their latest video products. With the Live API, users can go beyond phone cameras and use Facebook Live on professional cameras, multi-camera setups, and programmatic sources such as games or screencasts.

Facebook Page

Facebook pages are profiles that represent businesses, public figures, and brands. Facebook pages look and function similarly to regular Facebook profiles, except they have several capabilities that profiles do not have, such as boosting and scheduling posts, creating ads, and targeting an audience.

Facebook Pixel

A piece of JavaScript code that tracks the actions and locations of users in a website.

Facebook Search

Facebook's search engine that helps users find people, posts, photos, places, pages, groups, apps, and events, among numerous others.

Fan

In page insights and other places on Facebook, the term "fan" refers to the people who like or follow your page. These people are also referred to as followers.

Follow

A follow is an action that occurs when a user either likes or follows a page or a profile or adds another user as a friend. When a user follows a page or a person, that user will see the posts of the person or the page on news feed.

Free Basics

A Facebook platform that provides free, basic access to websites that are otherwise difficult to access with basic Internet services. Users can easily access information news related to maternal health, travel, local jobs, sports, communication, and the local government.

Frequency

The average number of times an ad was shown to each user.

Friends of Fans

A targeting option that allows advertisers to target individuals who are friends with people who follow or like the advertisers' pages.

G

Gift Sale Conversion Value

The total value returned from the gift sale conversions as a result of an ad.

Gift Sales

The number of gifts sold on Facebook as a result of an ad.

Groups

Facebook groups are private spaces where users can share interests and passions with other users who aren't on their friends list. Users can post statuses and share documents, photos, and videos in groups. Currently, selling used items is the most popular use for Facebook groups.

I

Impressions

The number of times an ad is displayed on a user's screen.

Instagram Stories

Instagram Stories is a feature that allows users to share ephemeral, twenty-four-hour videos and photos that vanish forever a day after the post was posted.

Instant Articles

Instant Articles is a Facebook feature that allows publishers' articles to quickly and easily load and open within its app. Instant Articles is also a placement option for Facebook ads.

Interest Targeting

Interest targeting is a targeting option that allows advertisers to target an audience with particular interests such as activities, music, movies, and TV shows.

K

Key Web Page Views (Conversion)

The number of times users viewed a key page on a website as a result of an ad.

L

Landing Page

A landing page is a single web page that users arrive to after clicking an ad.

Lead Ad

A lead ad, a Facebook ad type, is a digital form that collects users' information. Lead ads are typically used to collect contact information to grow leads. The most common information collected are first and last name, phone number, and email address.

Lead Magnet

A valuable offer advertisers give to potential customers in exchange for their personal information.

Leads (Conversion)

A lead is a potential customer who responded to a lead ad and gave the advertiser his or her contact information. When analyzing data, it can also refer to the number of new leads acquired as a result of an ad.

Leads Conversion Value

The total value returned from acquiring new leads as a result of an ad.

Lifetime Budget

A lifetime budget is the amount advertisers spend over the lifetime of an ad set.

Like

Liking is an action that occurs on Facebook when users click on the like button, symbolized by Facebook's thumbs-up icon.

Like Sources

A metric, which can be found within page insights, shows the number of times users liked a Facebook page within a specified date range.

Liked by Page

A section on Facebook that features all of the other pages that another page liked.

Link Ads

Link ads contain CTA buttons that direct users to a website.

Link Clicks

The number of link clicks on an ad or page that direct users off Facebook as a result of an ad (e.g., clicks to install an app, to view an off-site video, and to visit another website).

Lookalike Audiences

An audience that closely resembles a target audience. Advertisers create Lookalike Audiences by uploading a Custom Audience to Facebook.

M

Marquee Campaigns

A premium product for Instagram advertisers that helps drive mass awareness and expand reach in a short period of time. Advertisers usually use marquee campaigns for movie premieres and product launches.

Media Consumption

The number of times users clicked and viewed media content advertisers published on their pages on a specific day.

Messenger

A Facebook standalone app that lets users send instant messages to friends.

Messenger Bots

AI technology that functions as an automated response tool for businesses with Facebook pages.

Mixed Values

In Ads Manager and Power Editor, mixed values, also known as multiple values, indicate that a value for a field is not identical cross the campaigns, ad sets, or ads an advertiser is editing.

Mobile App Achievements

The number of levels achieved in a mobile app as a result of an ad.

Mobile App Actions

The number of actions that occurred in a mobile app as a result of an ad.

Mobile App Actions Conversion Value

The total value returned from actions that occurred in a mobile app as a result of an ad.

Mobile App Add-to-Cart

The number of times customers added an item to a shopping cart in a mobile app as a result of an ad.

Mobile App Adds-to-Cart Conversion Value

The total value returned from items added to a cart in an app as a result of an ad. The value is based on the value assigned to the conversion type in the pixel code.

Mobile App Adds-to-Wish list

The number of times something was added to a wish list in an app as a result of an ad.

Mobile App Adds-to-Wish list Conversion Value

The total value returned from items added to a wish list in an app as a result of an ad. This is based on the value assigned to the conversion type in the pixel code.

Mobile App Checkouts

The number of checkouts initiated in an app as a result of an ad.

Mobile App Checkouts Conversion Value

The total value returned from checkouts initiated in a mobile app as a result of an ad. This is based on the value assigned to the conversion type in the pixel code.

Mobile App Content Views

The number of content views in an app as a result of an ad.

Mobile App Content Views Conversion Value

The total value returned from content views in your mobile app as a result of your ad. This is based on the value assigned to the conversion type in your pixel code.

Mobile App Credit Spends

The number of times advertising coupons were spent in your mobile app as a result of your ad.

Mobile App Feature Unlocks

The number of features, levels, or achievements users unlocked in a mobile app as a result of an ad.

Mobile App Payment Details

The number of times payment information was entered in a mobile app as a result of an ad.

Mobile App Purchases

The number of times users purchased in app as a result of an ad.

Mobile App Purchases Conversion Value

The total value returned from purchases made in a mobile app as a result of an ad. This is based on the value assigned to the conversion type in the pixel code.

Mobile App Ratings

The number of ratings in your mobile app as a result of your ad.

Mobile App Ratings Conversion Value

The total value returned from ratings in a mobile app as a result of an ad. This is based on the value assigned to the conversion type in the pixel code.

Mobile App Registrations

The number of mobile app registrations as a result of an ad.

Mobile App Searches

The number of searches in a mobile app as a result of an ad.

Mobile App Starts

The number of mobile app starts as a result of an ad.

Mobile App Tutorial Completions

The number of tutorials completed in an app as a result of an ad.

Monthly Active Users

This is the number of people who have viewed or interacted with a Facebook page during the previous thirty days.

Multicultural Affinity

In targeting, this is a term that describes users who are interested in and likely to respond well to multicultural content. Targeting is based on affinity, not ethnicity.

N

Native Advertising

On Facebook, native advertising is a type of disguised online advertising in which marketers create ads that match the look, tone, and function of regular, unpaid posts.

Net Likes

The difference between the number of people who have liked a page and the number of people who have unliked a page over a specific time period.

New Likes

The total number of unique users who liked a Facebook page during a specific time period.

News Feed

News feed, a scrollable trail of posts, is the main part of Facebook where the posts of friends, family, followed pages, and ads appear.

Notes

A feature that lets users publish messages in rich-text format.

Notifications

Updates about activity on Facebook that a user is involved in. For example, users can receive notifications if someone commented on their posts or a post that they previously commented on. They can also receive reaction, birthday, and saved post notifications, among many others.

O

Objective

The goal for a Facebook ad. Objectives include traffic, engagement, lead generation, and video views, among numerous others.

Offer

A discount or digitized coupon code users can claim from a Facebook ad.

Offer Claimed Story

A sponsored story highlighting users who have claimed a Facebook offer.

Offer Claims

The number of claims on an offer as a result of an ad.

Optimizing for App Events

An optimization and pricing option available in Power Editor and Ads API for mobile app engagement ads that optimizes an ad for users most likely to complete an app event.

Organic Reach

Organic reach is the number of unique individuals who saw a specific post from a page on their news feeds or from the page itself.

Other Clicks

A metric that measures clicks on page titles to see more, not clicks on a page's content.

Other Mobile App Actions

The number of other actions in your mobile app as a result of your ad.

Other Website Conversion Value

The total value returned from other conversions on a website as a result of an ad.

Other Website Conversions

The number of other conversions on a website as a result of an ad.

P

Page Admin

The highest role assigned for a Facebook page. Page admins have the most capabilities, from assigning new roles and changing page settings to adding or removing other page contributors.

Page Engagement

The number of engagements on a page and a page's posts as a result of an ad.

Page Like Story

A sponsored story that features users who liked a page.

Page Likes

The number of likes on your page as a result of an ad.

Page Mentions

The number of mentions of a page as a result of an ad.

Page Post Ad

A regular post from a page that an advertiser turns into an ad in Ads Manager or Power Editor.

Page Post Sponsored Story

An ad that promotes the interaction (e.g., like or comment) of a target user's friend with the advertiser's page post.

Page Roles

A function assumed by a person managing a Facebook page. Roles include admin, editor, moderator, advertiser, and analyst.

Page Tab Views

The number of tab views on a page as a result of an ad.

Page Tabs

Buttons that mark pages that users can click and open.

Page Views

The total number of times users viewed a Facebook page during a period of time.

Paid Reach

This is the number of unique individuals who saw a specific post from your page through a paid source such as a Facebook Ad or Promoted Post.

Partner Categories

Targeting options Facebook's third-party partners provide. The targeting options under partner categories are taken from third-party data on offline behaviors.

Payment Methods

Verified forms of payment added to an ad account.

People Taking Action

The number of unique users who took an action (e.g., liking a page or installing an app) as a result of an ad.

Photo Views

The number of photo views as a result of an ad.

Pixel Helper

A Chrome extension that helps advertisers check whether their Facebook pixel is working properly on any website.

Placement

The location where ads will appear. Placements include desktop news feed, mobile news feed, and Audience Network, among many others.

Post Comments

The number of comments on a page's posts as a result of an ad.

Post Engagement

The number of actions (e.g., likes, comments, shares, photo views, link clicks, and video views) related to a page's posts as a result of your ad.

Post Feedback

The number of likes and comments on posts published from a page during the time period selected.

Post Reach

This is the number of people who have seen your post. You post counts as reaching someone when it's shown in their news feed. Figures displayed in Insights are for the first twenty-eight days after a post was created and include people viewing your post on desktop and mobile.

Post Shares

The number of post shares as a result of an ad.

Post Views

The number of times a story published on your Facebook page news feed was viewed during the time period you select.

Posts to Page

Posts to page are posts posted on a page by someone other than an admin.

Potential Reach

The number of monthly active people on Facebook that match the audience defined through audience targeting selections.

Power Editor

Power Editor is a page within Business Manager that allows advertisers to simultaneously edit multiple ads at once.

Primary Payment Method

The default payment method for an ad account.

Profile

Facebook users' personal pages that detail their personal information, posting activity, and interactions with other users. Profiles, which cannot be used for commercial use, can either be public or private.

R

Reach

The total number of users who saw an advertiser's ad.

Registrations (Conversion)

The number of times users registered on a website as a result of an ad.

Registrations Conversion Value

The total value returned from completed registrations on a website as a result of an ad.

Relevance Score

The relevance score estimates an ad's relevance to its target audience in real time.

Reports

Reports are the documentation of the most important ad metrics that show how an advertiser is reaching his or her business goals.

Result Rate

The number of results received divided by the number of impressions.

Results

The number of actions as a result of an ad. The results shown are based on the objective.

S

Social Click Rate

The number of social clicks divided by social impressions.

Social Clicks

Clicks on ads displayed to users as social proof.

Social Clicks (All)

The number of clicks on ads (e.g., likes, reactions, and shares) displayed to users as social proof.

Social Impressions

The number of times an ad that highlighted its engagement was displayed in front of users.

Social Plug-ins

Buttons that users can install into their websites. The buttons allow users to share their experiences off Facebook with their friends on Facebook. Clicking the share-to-Facebook button from a website to share an article is one example.

Social Reach

The number of users who saw an ad that highlighted its engagement.

Source Audience

A source audience is an audience advertisers derive their Lookalike Audience from. Page fans and Custom Audience are examples of a source audience.

Start Date

The day a campaign starts.

Status

The current state of ad sets and ads. Ads can show a status of on, off, running, paused, completed, or deleted.

Suggested Bid Range

A bid range that Facebook suggests to advertisers to ensure that their ads receive the right amount of impressions.

T

Tagging

An action that links a person or page to something a user posts, whether that is a photo, a status, or a check-in.

Ten-Second Video Views

The number of times users have viewed your video for ten seconds. If your video is less than ten seconds, then this refers to the number of times people viewed 97 percent of your video.

Thirty-Second Video Views

The number of times users have viewed your video for thirty seconds. If your video is thirty seconds or less, then this refers to the number of times people viewed 97 percent of your video.

Ticker

The ticker is a bar on the right side of Facebook desktop that updates users of their friends' activities in real time.

Timeline

The timeline, located front and center on a Facebook profile, is a scrollable trail of posts that a user or a friend of a user posted. Tagged posts and life events also appear on the timeline.

Timeline Review

A privacy setting that allows users to approve or reject posts that they have been tagged in or posts that friends want to post on their timeline.

Top Stories

Top stories, which Facebook's algorithm thinks is relevant to a user, appear on top of a user's news feed. Posts that have a high score in Facebook's algorithm will appear higher in news feed.

Total Conversion Value

The total revenue returned from conversions or Facebook credit spends that occurred on a website or an app. This is based on the value assigned to the conversion type in the pixel code.

Trademark

A trademark is a word, slogan, symbol, or logo that identifies and distinguishes the products or services offered by one party from those offered by others.

Trending

A small box on the right side of Facebook desktop that features a list of topics that have recently spiked in popularity on Facebook.

U

Unique Clicks (All)

The total number of unique users who clicked on an ad. For example, if ten people click on the same ad five times, the ad will have ten unique clicks.

Unique CTR (All)

A value calculated by dividing the number of people who clicked anywhere in an ad by the number of people reached. For example, if an ad that was shown to 1,000 users received ten unique clicks, the unique CTR would be 1 percent.

Unlikes

In analytics, the number of unique users who unliked a page during a specified date range.

Unpublished Page Post

An unpublished page post, also known as a dark post, is a post created in Power Editor that will not immediately appear in news feed and pages, allowing advertisers to create an ad for that post without publishing it to the public.

V

Verification Hold

A temporary charge on an advertiser's account used to validate a credit card. The $1.01 charge will be removed from the credit card within three to five business days.

Verified Page

A Facebook page that has been verified by Facebook as authentic. Verified pages contain a check mark alongside their names.

Video Ads

Video ads are ad formats that, when clicked, play a video.

Video Views

The number of times users viewed a video for three seconds or more.

Video Views to 25 Percent

The number of times users viewed a video to 25 percent of its length, including views that skipped to that point.

Video Views to 50 Percent

The number of times users viewed a video to 50 percent of its length, including views that skipped to that point.

Video Views to 75 Percent

The number of times users viewed a video to 75 percent of its length, including views that skipped to that point.

Video Views to 95 Percent

The number of times users viewed a video to 95 percent of its length, including views that skipped to that point.

Viral Reach

Viral reach is the number of unique users who saw a page post from a story published by one of their Facebook friends.

Virtual Reality

Technology that creates an immersive, simulated 3-D environment.

W

Website Action Value (All)

The total value of the actions tracked by a Facebook pixel on a website after users clicked an ad.

Website Actions (All)

The total number of actions tracked by a Facebook pixel on a website after users clicked ad.

ABOUT THE AUTHOR

Brian Meert is the founder and CEO of AdvertiseMint, a Facebook advertising agency that he created in 2014 after discovering Facebook's revolutionary advertising platform while working as the VP of marketing for a financial company. After seeing Facebook's potential to dominate digital advertising, Brian abandoned his nine-to-five job, went home, and started his company.

Before becoming the CEO of AdvertiseMint, Brian, who has an MBA in marketing from La Sierra University, built and sold Gofobo, worked as the VP of marketing for American Bullion and JobSync, and held a director of marketing position at Fremont College. Brian has been in advertising for fifteen years, starting his first digital advertising campaign in 2003 with his cafeteria money.

When Brian isn't answering phone calls from clients, holding team meetings, and teaching classes at General Assembly, you will find him tanning at the beach with his brown, curly-haired dog, Sophie, taking big bites out of his favorite food, a peanut butter and jelly sandwich.

Made in the USA
Middletown, DE
12 March 2018